John Henry Ingram

**Oliver Madox Brown**

A Biographical Sketch, 1855-1874

John Henry Ingram

**Oliver Madox Brown**
*A Biographical Sketch, 1855-1874*

ISBN/EAN: 9783337028374

Printed in Europe, USA, Canada, Australia, Japan

Cover: Foto ©Thomas Meinert / pixelio.de

More available books at **www.hansebooks.com**

# *OLIVER MADOX BROWN.*

## A Biographical Sketch.

### 1855—1874.

BY
JOHN H. INGRAM.

LONDON:
ELLIOT STOCK, 62, PATERNOSTER ROW, E.C.
1883.

TO

## HIS PARENTS

THESE MEMORIALS OF

# OLIVER MADOX BROWN

ARE INSCRIBED BY

THEIR COLLECTOR.

# INTRODUCTION.

'I AM sure that no memoir will ever do Oliver justice,' wrote Mr. Richard Garnett to the youth's father some months ago: 'The wonderful precocity of his genius may be set forth, but the peculiar charm of his character, its sweetness and manliness, its alliance of the most daring originality to the most exquisite ingenuousness, can never be adequately represented, even by those who knew him most intimately. It was something unique and indescribable, and the objective and purely imaginative character of his writings renders even them very inadequate exponents of his mind and heart. I should despair of communicating any just conception of him to one who never knew him, and can only say that I should expect anything sooner than to meet with another Oliver Madox Brown.'

Confronted by this opinion, and by the fact that, personally, Oliver Madox Brown was unknown to me, my attempt to compile a short biography of him will appear to savour of rashness. I was, however, prompted to the undertaking, not only by admiration for his genius, but by the circumstance that whilst every year lessened the material for a faithful record, no effort appeared to be made by any of his personal friends to produce one; and that no fuller *Memoir* existed of him than the few pages prefixed to his *Literary Remains;* to which, to Mr. P. B. Marston's article on 'Oliver Madox Brown' in *Scribner's Magazine,* and to an appreciative, able critique on the *Literary Remains* in the *Examiner,* I am indebted for various items of value. My researches have been so warmly and generously aided by the friends and relatives of the talented youth, and so many interesting *data* have been forthcoming, that I am not altogether hopeless of having obtained a sufficiency and excellency of material to attract even those who, like myself, were personally unacquainted with Oliver Madox Brown.

Indeed, whatever interest appertains to this monograph is due to the kind assistance afforded me by those who knew and loved the youthful author: I am little more than the compiler and editor of their communications. To Mr. Ford Madox Brown my warmest thanks are due for kind permission to make full use of his son's correspondence and poems (published and unpublished), as also for information and corrections in matters of fact, and, above all, for the use of the illustrations to this volume; to Mrs. William M. Rossetti I am under deep obligation for valuable assistance; to Mr. William M. Rossetti I am much beholden for the use of Dante Rossetti's correspondence with Oliver, and to Mr. Philip B. Marston I am greatly indebted for his kindness in placing at my disposal some most interesting correspondence with his deceased friend, and for various items of information. My thanks are also tendered to Mrs. Robertson for the use of the letters addressed by Oliver to her father, the late Mr. W. Smith Williams, and to Mr. W. Theodore Watts, Mr. John Payne, Dr. T. Gordon Hake, Miss Mathilde Blind, Mr. E. R. Hughes, Monsieur V. Barthe, and all others who have generously aided my work by the presentation of original poems; the use of correspondence; personal information; and similar assistance.

JOHN H. INGRAM.

# CONTENTS.

| CHAPTER | PAGE |
|---|---|
| I. CHILDHOOD | 1 |
| II. DAWNINGS OF GENIUS | 21 |
| III. THE BLACK SWAN | 45 |
| IV. GABRIEL DENVER | 67 |
| V. FRIENDSHIP | 93 |
| VI. LIFE IN LONDON AND LECHLADE | 123 |
| VII. THE DWALE BLUTH | 167 |
| VIII. DEATH'S FINAL CONQUEST | 217 |

## CHILDHOOD.

# Untimely Lost.

## OLIVER MADOX BROWN.
### Born 1855.  Died 1874.

Upon the landscape of his coming life
   A youth high-gifted gazed, and found it fair :
   The height of work, the floods of praise, were there.
What friendships, what desires, what love, what wife ?—
All things to come.  The fanned springtide was rife
   With imminent solstice ; and the ardent air
   Had summer sweets and autumn fires to bear ;—
Heart's ease full-pulsed with perfect strength for strife.

A mist has risen : we see the youth no more :
   Does *he* see on and strive on ?  And may we
   Late-tottering world worn hence, find *his* to be
The young strong hand which helps us up that shore ?
Or, echoing the No More with Nevermore,
   Must Night be ours and his ?  We hope : and he ?

Dante Gabriel Rossetti.

## CHAPTER I.

*CHILDHOOD.*

ADVOCATES of the theory that genius is hereditary are justified in referring to the ancestry of Oliver Madox Brown. His great-grandfather, founder of the 'Brunonian system,' was scarcely more celebrated in later life for his medical skill than in his youth he was noted for his scholastic precocity. Dr. John Brown left offspring who, if they did not rival their parent in genius, certainly upheld the family reputation for talent. One son, the editor of his father's works and the author of his biography, was Dr. William Cullen Brown, President of the Royal Medical Society of Edinburgh, and a distinguished scholar, whilst another son, Mr. Ford Brown, a Commissary in the Navy, was richly endowed with natural gifts. Mr. Ford Madox Brown, the well-known and most original artist, is son of the latter, and father of Oliver Madox Brown.

Oliver was born at Finchley on the 20th of January, 1855. More fortunate in his lot than the children of genius usually are, his lines were cast in pleasant places. From his birth he was surrounded by friends and relatives capable of both fostering and comprehending any traces of talent he might exhibit, so it is not surprising to discover that his earliest manifestations of precocity were thoroughly appreciated and lovingly treasured up in the memories of those about him. When but two years of age he made his first acquaintance with death; and the loss of a baby-brother—whom his elder sister found him weeping and lamenting in the nursery, crying out in the bitterness of his own baby heart, 'Arthur! Arthur! shall I never see you again?'—seems to have left an indelible impression upon his mind, as towards the close of his own brief career he spoke of it as the *earliest recollection* of his child-life.

Reared in so rare a forcing-ground as was his parents' home, little Oliver speedily displayed signs of hereditary genius, and many are the significant anecdotes and remarks related by his

OLIVER MADOX BROWN.
AT THE AGE OF FIVE,
FROM A PICTURE CALLED THE ENGLISH BOY, BY F. MADOX BROWN.

relatives in proof of his innate cleverness. For instance, it is recollected how one day, before he had completed his fourth year, he gave to a friend of the family so shrewd and critical a description of a landscape of 'Walton-on-the-Naze' painted by his father, that the visitor declared he felt as astounded as if 'the cat had taken to speaking.'

Amongst other interesting items told of his early childhood is that, whilst still in his fifth year, Oliver 'would cover the white marble mantel-shelves, and any other available spaces, with designs of hunts, battles, or subjects of that sort.' The same authority informs us that between the age of five and six the little lad stubbornly resisted being taught to read, 'yet set himself most sedulously to acquire any other knowledge that apparently did not concern him, but especially facts relating to natural history.' It was at this point of his brief career that his portrait as *The English Boy* was painted in oils by his father. Oliver, or 'Nolly' as he was always termed in his own circle, is portrayed with such characteristic emblems of childhood in his hands as whipping-top and whip, but, intentionally or not, so earnest and deep-thoughted an expression has been given to the beautiful face, that the toys seem less appropriate as playthings than as artistic accessories. The steady gazing eyes see something beyond the ken of conventional children, whilst the shapely nose and decided oval of the face give the countenance a definiteness of expression rarely beheld in one so young, and clearly foreshadow the future, but scarcely more set, features of the youth. Only in the delicate curves of the lips is beheld the one trait that grows less definite in after life.

Under his father's careful instruction, and impelled by the artistic incentives by which he was environed, Oliver continued to make good progress in painting, and by the age of eight had completed his first picture in water-colours. For ordinary routine study he does not appear to have exhibited much inclination, not, indeed, that any particular pressure was put upon him. At this period he was quite known in the neighbourhood for his extraordinary success in obtaining possession of small field animals, especially mice: these he usually kept in the lining of his jacket, through which they used to eat their way, to the annoyance and despair of his mother.

Even as a child he was deemed an acute physiognomist, and a very early instance of his shrewdness in this respect is remembered. When he was between seven and eight years of age his mother was needing a cook: young Oliver availed himself of an opportunity to inspect the candidates, and looked hard in the face of one of them for so long a time that at last she said to him, 'Well, master, what do you think of me?'

'You will stop here seven years,' he answered. And so she did.

The child's remark evidently impressed her, for at the expiration of the first seven years she remembered it, and said to him, 'Master Nolly, you said I should stay seven years, and here I am; what next?'

'Now you may stop another seven,' was the lad's rejoinder. And she is still with Oliver's parents, after a period of nearly thrice seven years' service.

In September, 1863, Oliver had his first genuine experience of the sea. He had been staying with his mother at Tynemouth, near Newcastle-on-Tyne, and it was arranged for them to return to London by steamboat. The windows of the house where they were staying overlooked the German Ocean, and enabled the inmates to discern the ominous appearance of the weather. Mrs. Madox Brown, however, determined to undertake the journey, although implored up to the very last moment not to risk

a voyage with the child in such weather. About
five o'clock in the evening the steamer crossed
the bar of the Tyne, when the full fury of the
storm at once broke around her; the wind blew
a hurricane, the rain poured in torrents, the
thunder roared overhead, whilst as the gloom
increased the lightning grew vivid and continuous. Swept by spray and rain, the deck was
neither comfortable nor safe, and all the passengers went below save Mrs. Madox Brown and
her son. Cradled in a coil of rope on the fore-
castle, for a long time the little fellow remained
intently absorbed in the grandeur of the scene,
too interested in it to feel afraid. Succumbing
at last to sea-sickness, he was persuaded by the
sailors to be carried down to his berth. The
next day the storm continued, and all the following night the vessel had to lie-to in the wash of
the Humber, afraid to steam ahead, it even being
doubtful where they were, nothing being discernible in the gloom but the white-crested
mountainous black waves. The engines got out
of order, rockets were fired, and altogether
matters seemed to have reached a dangerous
pass. Eventually, however, the state of affairs
improved, and after all the steamer reached the
Thames in safety. Mr. Madox Brown waited
vainly for many hours at St. Katherine's Wharf

in a state of anxiety that may well be imagined; but it was not until long past midnight of the third night that the weary travellers reached their home in the Highgate Road, having disembarked at Tilbury, and finished their journey by train. The wind was still howling round the house, and still furiously tossing the trees in the Grove. The influence of this voyage on the imaginative temperament of such a child as Oliver would be intense and lasting, providing him in after life with valuable material for his literary productions.

In due course of time, Oliver entered the junior classes of University College, and is said to have been chiefly distinguished among his schoolfellows for his idleness. One day his father called on the late Rev. Mr. Case, then head master of the junior boys, respecting his son's laziness. Mr. Case expressed regret at the fact, remarking that Oliver was as gentlemanly and nice a boy as could be desired, and always gave very clever answers. He added that the boy would be better away from the school, and if carefully looked after he believed he would grow up to distinguish himself. A characteristic scene now took place. Oliver was sent for and lectured kindly and seriously by the master for his idleness and untidiness.

'You cannot deny,' said Mr. Case, 'that the visitors at their last inspection described you as the dirtiest boy in the school. What a disgrace that was for you.'

'Yes, sir,' replied Oliver; 'but just before the inspection some big boys had thrown me down in a puddle, so that I was splashed all over.'

'Ah, that is just you,' was the master's rejoinder; 'always such capital answers; but don't you see, my boy, you would not be known for your excellent excuses, were it not for you so constantly doing things that require excusing. There, you may go now.'

In the December of 1865, Mr. Madox Brown removed with his family to 37, Fitzroy Square, and in that house Oliver spent nearly the whole remainder of his short life. At this time his father took him from University College and provided instruction for him at home. As yet it was only in painting that he made any considerable progress, his first production of any note after leaving school being a water-colour of *Queen Margaret and the Robbers*. The subject, which had been selected for him by his father as a task, was thoroughly appropriate for so juvenile an artist; but Oliver's treatment of it, so far from being weak or puerile, was strikingly original and vigorous. The scene is depicted as taking place in the skirts of a forest, where, behind the thickly tangled boughs and bosky stems of great trees, the sun is setting with an angry glare. This little work, say the authors of the introductory memoir to Oliver's *Literary Remains*, 'which was executed almost entirely without Nature, but with great pains and study, exhibits choice colour and dramatic vitality in the heads, which, when examined minutely, for they are not half the size of a thumb-nail, are really surprising, compacted as they are of childish *naïveté* and vivid characterization; the young prince's head is, indeed, as unexceptionable as anything the painter might afterwards have achieved.' To this analysis may be added that the mingled expressions of princely pride, boyish courage, and struggle to suppress fear, are portrayed with a power of introspection that shows something more matured than mere promise. This water-colour, which became the property of Dante Rossetti, elicited flattering notice from the acute, kind-hearted painter-poet. There are in existence still earlier paintings by Oliver, notably one of *Centaurs Hunting*, executed before the artist was eleven years old; but naturally they are of inferior merit to that which invoked the appreciative criticism of Dante Gabriel Rossetti.

When about twelve years of age Oliver was taken to Southend, and whilst there beheld for the first time, as the rain swept across the smooth water of the Thames estuary, that phosphorescent glow of the sea which he afterwards made such effective use of in his initial romance of *The Black Swan:* it was one of those weird phenomena of nature so calculated to deeply impress a child of his excitable temperament and vivid imagination. A typical incident is related in connection with this sea-side visit. One night Oliver greatly alarmed his mother and sister by prolonging his boyish rambles until past eleven. He returned home with his clothes torn and dirty, but with a collection of glow-worms carefully tied up in his handkerchief. These insects were speedily transferred to a box, which was placed in their captor's room; but in the night they contrived to escape, and penetrated under the door into his mother's bedroom, much to her dismay, and to the no slight disgust of the landlady, whose proclivities towards natural history were not very strong. The next morning Oliver managed to recapture his entomological pets, and insisted upon retaining them until the evening, when, after dark, he deposited them upon a bush growing in the front-garden, where they formed a brilliant illumination, to the astonishment of the visitors and his own exceeding delight. In *The Dwale Bluth* Oliver made most effective use of this episode of his boyhood, as, indeed, he did of so many others, apparently basing all leading incidents of his works on the personal experiences of himself or of his friends.

Another picturesque, but somewhat hazardous, adventure appertains to the same year. A friend of Mr. Madox Brown gave a picnic on the Thames, in a flat-bottomed boat especially prepared for the occasion. About thirty guests, including Oliver, were invited and assembled at Southend, whence they sailed to the Nore and about the mouth of the river. The entertainment proved a complete success, and the whole party was very joyous. At sunset most of the company were sent home by way of Southend, but a few sailed back to Gravesend and spent the night there. The following day was passed on the water, and the night on shore at Herne Bay. The next morning all, including young Oliver, had to be on board by four o'clock in order to catch the tide; and a wonderful sail they had back to Southend. The breeze being brisk, and, in nautical phraseology 'full in their teeth,' they had to tack about to reach the estuary of the Thames. The wind having veered round in the night, hundreds of colliers that had been wind-bound for days met them on their journey, and in accordance with the rule of the sea had, each of them, to lie-to to let the barge pass; for a barge having only a captain and one boy for crew was literally helpless in such a crisis, and but for such a rule, might have been run into at any moment. The scene, with the bright morning sun level with the horizon, was magnificent, and with the spice of danger thrown in was quite exciting. The wind continued to blow fresh, and the barge, all open as had been arranged for the picnic, heeled over somewhat more than was desirable, but eventually made Southend and anchored in safety. Oliver and his host went on shore in the small boat to procure some milk for breakfast, but in rowing back to the barge the wind caught them and carried them out to sea. During their desperate efforts to row back, one of the rowlock-pins broke, and had they not been overtaken and rescued by a large cutter sent in pursuit of them, they must have drifted out helplessly to sea. It was in such stirring incidents as these that Oliver found material out of which to fashion, in after years, the realistic scenes of nautical life with which *The Black Swan* abounds.

Returned to Fitzroy Square, he resumed the

even tenor of his way, nothing more exciting happening, so far as our researches show, than the thinking out of poems and the working out ideas on canvas. Writing to his sister on the 26th of July, 1868, he said, 'I have begun painting my Jason picture: the colour has not come good at present, but I suppose it may come better when I get more of it in.' The painting thus referred to is a water-colour of *Chiron receiving the Infant Jason from the Slave;* the subject having been selected by the youthful artist himself. This work was exhibited in the Dudley Gallery, in 1869, and it may well be doubted, say the editors of the *Remains,* 'even leaving out of account the question of comparative merits, whether any other so juvenile painter ever offered, or obtained admission for, a work in that exhibition.' In the same year that he painted the Jason picture, Oliver drew some sketches of *Kittens,* now the property of Mr. E. R. Hughes, the artist. These sketches, though roughly executed, are quite remarkable for the knowledge of feline character they display: the difficulty of expressing traits of cat-life correctly is well known, and the happy way in which the young artist has caught and transferred the poses of his unruly sitters demonstrates at least his sympathetic acquaintance with animal life.

Some time in 1869 Oliver drew two designs for an edition of Byron's poems which his father was illustrating, and Mr. W. M. Rossetti editing, for Messrs. Moxons, and they were published with the other illustrations in the volume referred to. *Mazeppa*, one of these drawings, he afterwards painted in oils and exhibited at the New British Institution in 1871, whilst the other, illustrating a scene in the *Deformed Transformed*, he also commenced in oils but never completed. About the time he was painting his Jason picture he also made some sketches of which the ideas—if they had possessed no other merit—were certainly very remarkable for a lad: one of these tentatives represents two men rowing across a river and meeting the ghosts of all the people who had been drowned in it, walking in procession. Truly an extraordinary subject for a boy to conceive!

The summer of 1869 Oliver spent with his mother and younger sister (now Mrs. Hueffer), at Gorleston, a village on the mouth of the Yar, by Great Yarmouth. Yarmouth harbour is at the mouth of the river, where there are a couple of rough picturesque piers pushed out into the sea, one at each side of the river's junction with the ocean. Gorleston is a long quaint sort of village skirting the river and bounded by a series of shipbuilding yards, through each of which a right-of-way exists along the water's edge. Here the lad was quite at home, making friends with the sailors, and listening to their yarns about the sea and shipping, of which themes he was always delighted to hear. He appears to have been allowed, even at that early age, to follow out his own ways and inclinations, but one night his staying out was so prolonged that his mother became anxious, and he had to be sought for. He was finally discovered crossing and recrossing the ferry between the ship-building yards on the one side of the harbour and the race-course on the other, ruining himself in halfpenny journeys in order to study once more that phosphorescence of the water which had so greatly excited his boyish imagination two years before.

Whilst at Gorleston Oliver did not neglect his artistic studies. Writing to his elder sister, he says, 'For the last four or five days I have been making a sketch of the pier. It is not very pleasant drawing from the top of the cliffs, the weather has been so nasty, and the sand is blown into one's eyes so. When I went yesterday I found that a piece of the cliff, a few yards from where I had been sitting, had fallen away; there was a lump big enough to crush an ox on the sand underneath.' In another letter to his sister, referring to his view of the pier, he says, 'I almost received an offer for my sketch from two fishermen who, after looking over my shoulder for two or three minutes, at last made out that I was sketching the pier. One asked the other in a low tone what I should be likely to ask for it. His friend, however, muttered something that I did not hear, and dragged him away.'

Apparently Oliver did not get on so well with these men on all occasions. A number of fishermen were wont to watch him from the upper cliff, and one day they excited his anger by throwing small pieces of earth or turf at him. He climbed up the bank to them and demanded which of them had done it. They asked him what he intended doing to the culprit, and he replied, 'I want to throw him over the cliff!' Doubtless they thought he was a plucky boy, so they only looked at him, and at each other, but said nothing. He was, however, on very friendly terms with the man who had charge of the lighthouse at the pierhead, and often in rough weather they sat shut in together, talking over the secrets of the sea, whilst the waves washed over the jetty. The old salt would say to Mrs. Madox Brown, 'That's a very sharp lad of you'rn, marm.'

Another acquaintance Oliver made at Gorleston, and one from whom he doubtless obtained much of that quaint out-of-the-way information he sought for everywhere so diligently, was the old landlady's brother, an overseer of the poor. This man used to call for the lad, and take him long drives in his trap, probably beguiling the time by recounting many moving tales and showing many touching scenes of human misery.

One evening, after a long ramble alone, Oliver returned with a young duck under his coat, saying to his mother, 'See what I have brought you.' He had rescued the duckling from some boys who had tied it up and were pelting it with stones. At an expenditure of sixpence he had preserved the poor bird from its tormentors, who had doubtless stolen it, as the old landlady insisted; she objected to its being brought into the house, declaring the police would come and search the premises for it shortly. But Oliver maintained that he had bought it honestly, and would not give it up, and after a few days the landlady became reconciled to her new lodger. On its arrival the duckling was put in a cupboard, whence it was afterwards taken to be placed with some chickens in a hen-house. At first the chickens were afraid of the new arrival, but no sooner did they discover its harmlessness than with a malignity perfectly human they began to peck it. Oliver then transferred the poor foundling to a tub of water, where the poor bird revived and throve, and where it was still enjoying life when its youthful preserver left Gorleston.

*DAWNINGS OF GENIUS.*

## In Remembrance of Nolly Brown.

Not a gift did he lose in that passage of night
When so young he escaped to the skies overhead!
We look for him there, who no longer is dead,
But returns to our eyes in a likeness of light.
Hope ever is true when it comes from a height,
And tells us that we the free passage shall gain,
To rejoin him we love on the measureless plain,
Where travellers long parted once more come in sight.
And Nolly was never so near as to-day,
Far off as he seemed at that sorrowful end,
But the distance fast dwindles, we tarry half-way,
We press on again to recover our friend;
New prospects there open that once coldly lay
In the earth-depths but now to the sky-depths extend.

THOMAS GORDON HAKE.

*April,* 1883.

## CHAPTER II.

### *DAWNINGS OF GENIUS.*

THE year 1869 was a memorable one in the life of Oliver, from the circumstance that therein was revealed to his family the fact that he was a poet. The name of poet is not used in any careless or irreverential mood, but as fitly applied to the lad who, at the age of fourteen, was enabled to produce such artistic and richly worded verse as, from the specimens preserved to us, we know his to have been. At the age mentioned Oliver permitted six or seven sonnets he had written to be seen by some of his relatives; they were greatly surprised at this revelation, as until then it had not even been surmised that he had so much as understood what a 'sonnet' was. Eventually, with one exception, the whole of these juvenile poems were supposed to have perished, their youthful author having destroyed them 'in a fit of morbid irritability or bashfulness caused by their being shown to a few friends.' The solitary sonnet believed to have escaped destruction owed its preservation to the fact of its having been printed on the frame of a picture by Mrs. Stillman (then Miss Spartali), for which it had been composed as a motto. This poem, written when its author was only thirteen years of age, has already been published in the *Literary Remains* of Oliver Madox Brown, but as a specimen of his precocious skill in word-painting, and as the earliest known evidence of his poetic powers extant, must be adduced here, and in the form given on the gilt picture-frame; our *variorum* readings having been obtained from a recently discovered manuscript copy by the author:

### SONNET.

Leaning against the window, rapt in thought,
  Of what sweet past do thy soft brown\* eyes dream
  That so expressionlessly sweet they seem?
Or what great image hath thy fancy wrought
To wonder round and gaze at? Or doth aught
  Of legend move thee, o'er which eyes oft stream,
  Telling of some sweet saint who rose supreme
From martyrdom to God, with glory fraught?
Or art thou listening to the gondolier,
  Whose song is dying o'er the waters wide,
Trying the faintly-sounding tune to hear
  Before it mixes with the rippling tide?
Or dost thou think of one that † comes not near,
  And whose false heart, in thine, thine own doth chide?

---

\* Fair grey.      † Who.

There is little in these lines a matured poet need hesitate to own, but when it is remembered that they are the production of a boy of thirteen, wonder and admiration are alike excited. Few poets have produced anything worthy preservation prior to their assumption of the *toga virilis*, and, taking into consideration his lowly surroundings and defective education, Chatterton may be deemed unique among bards, inasmuch as his hapless career was ended at so early an age. But Oliver Madox Brown, despite the peculiarly felicitous incentives by which he was environed, may be considered as marvellously precocious as a poet. The sonnet just cited has many claims for our admiration, but to us it appears to be far out-rivalled in virility of thought—in picturesque originality—by another sonnet Oliver wrote somewhere about the same time, but the manuscript of which has only recently been discovered. This poem, which has never been published, reads thus:

### SONNET.

Made indistinguishable 'mid the boughs,
  With saddened weary ever-restless eyes
 ·The weird Chameleon of the past world lies,
Like some old wretched man whom God allows
To linger on : still joyless life endows
  His wasted frame, and memory never dies
  Within him, and his only sympathies
Withered with his last comrade's last carouse.

> Methinks great Dante knew thee not of old,
>   Else some fierce glutton all insatiate
>   Compelled within some cage for food to wait
> He must have made thee, and his verse have told
>   How thou in vain thy ravening tried'st to sate
> On flylike souls of triflers overbold.

There is something truly grandiose and weird in the idea enunciated by the first eight lines of this sonnet. The likening of a surviving member of the past world's inhabitants to an old reveller who has outlived all his joys, his comrades, and his sympathies, is not only very striking, but is very unlike what would have been looked for in the work of a boy.

There exists yet another sonnet by Oliver Madox Brown, which has been prefixed to Chapter IV., entitled *Gabriel Denver*. It is certainly not one of the six or seven supposed to have been destroyed, and, doubtless, belongs to a somewhat later date in its author's career; but as this is a matter difficult to unravel, it is as well to refer readers to it, so that it may be perused in conjunction with the other similarly constructed poems.*

Although this sonnet was found prefixed to the first manuscript copy of its author's earliest known prose work, it does not necessarily follow that it was coeval in date of composition with

---

* Vide p. 68.

*The Black Swan*, especially as we are informed that that romance was originally 'thought out' when Oliver was only fifteen years of age.

The strict suppression of expletives, and the happy rhymes which characterize these sonnets, are the least of their merits, their chief beauty, indeed, being due to their author's pictorial experience, which enabled him to endow them with vitalizing ideas, and to fully realize for us Coleridge's exquisite conception, ' My eyes make pictures when they are shut.'

The composition of verses does not seem to have diverted Oliver's attention from his other artistic pursuits. About the time that the premature exposition of his poetry excited his wrath, he appears to have been devoting himself most diligently to his pencil and palette. At this period equestrian subjects found chief favour in his eyes, among the most notable of the productions painted whilst their influence lasted being a water-colour, styled *Obstinacy*, which was exhibited in 1870 at the Dudley Gallery, where its merits attracted the attention of Mr. King, of Liverpool, by whom it was purchased. It is a picture full of life and action, representing a horse, the rider of which is strenuously endeavouring to urge the snorting, stubborn brute through the waves as they break foaming on the shore. *Exercise*, a companion painting, was exhibited the same year at the Royal Academy by the young artist: it is described as the portrayal of a groom 'galloping an Arab horse round and round in the firm sand of the sea-shore, "taking the spirit out of him," to the music of the tumbling breakers.'

No more work of any pretension is recorded to have been completed until the following year, although a very large number of studies of various kinds belong to this period, and prove that Oliver was not neglecting his artistic pursuits. During the summer of 1870 he again visited Gorleston, and would appear from his correspondence to have depicted the quaint old pier anew; but no striking incidents are recorded of his stay this time. Oliver now became very nearsighted, to which circumstance he was wont to allude in ludicrously exaggerated terms. One day, when visiting his friend, John Payne, the poet, he contrived to march off with his host's gold glasses; reminded of this by letter, he replied, 'I am proud to say that I *did* succeed in carrying off your spectacles; but, alas! there are some victories which are worse than defeats. They are so strong that they nearly wrung my eyes out when I tried to wear them the next day. You shall have them back again to-morrow.'

Eccentric from his earliest childhood, some of Oliver's peculiarities now began to grow very marked, amongst others being his treatment of his watch, a fairly good gold one, which he had purchased upon the sale of one of his pictures, either *Obstinacy* or *Jason*. After he had been the owner of this watch for a short time, he relinquished, beyond all power of inducement, the task of winding it up. He seemed to like to wear the watch, but the exertion of winding it up soon became intolerable, and even the trouble of detaching the guard from his waistcoat button-hole at night was too much for him. Nevertheless he continued to wear the watch long after the interior had become, by rough usage, a complete wreck. A watchmaker, who was eventually spoken to about putting the article in good going order, began to laugh, declaring that nothing but a new inside would ever effect that. The watch was left in its crippled condition, and remains so to this day.

The records of this portion of Oliver's career are necessarily scanty, and relate chiefly to his artistic labours. The principal painting he had as yet produced was of a scene from *The Tempest*, a scene admirably suited for pictorial representation, but, it is supposed, never previously painted. The picture, a water-colour, was displayed at the

International Exhibition at South Kensington, in 1871. It was of *Prospero and the Infant Miranda* being sent adrift in 'a rotten carcase of a boat,' by the hired traitors of the usurping Duke of Milan, as related by Prospero to his daughter (Act 1, Scene ii.). This painting, which invoked high praise for its originality and power, was eventually purchased by Mr. Rowley, of Manchester, and by him, after it's artist's death, was generously presented to Mr. Madox Brown.

In the summer of 1871 Oliver spent five weeks at Lynnmouth, Devonshire, and whilst there painted a water-colour of the river Lynn, much provoking his father, however, by leaving it unfinished and going off on the last day of his visit to see Exmoor. This desertion seemed quite unreasonable at the time, but the use which he subsequently made of the local knowledge thus hastily gained is well known to readers of *The Dwale Bluth*.

During a portion of 1871 and the two succeeding years, Oliver, in company with several like-minded young men, attended a life-class held at a studio or *atélier* at Chelsea. The studio belonged to a Frenchman named Barthe, an amateur enamoured of the artistic career, and was started and maintained on the same system

PROSPERO & MIRANDA.

as that of Suisse, in Paris. Each of the students —and Monsieur Barthe soon gathered several earnest young men about him—paid a small sum towards defraying the expenses, but the proprietor, or rather originator, of the class could not have realized much, if any, profit from the enterprise. But Monsieur Barthe was an artist himself, and thoroughly enjoyed these *noctes ambrosianæ*, if so they may be designated. An artistic wardrobe for lending to the students was being gradually gathered together, and a new and more suitable studio than that they originally met in was built for the purposes of the class, which was really for the professional study of the nude.

After the two *lustra* or so which have elapsed since Oliver attended at this *atélier*, it is somewhat difficult to obtain much information about the work he did there, yet one or two of the students, and some of them are now distinguished men, have been found able and willing to furnish reminiscences of what the place and its frequenters were like at that time. One gentleman, who recalls to mind what a favourite Oliver had made himself by his great good-heartedness and his brilliant wit, remembers taking a walk with him and a third student from Chelsea to Newman Street, but thinks the walk was only remarkable for a persistent drizzling rain, and for Mr. N—— wearing his hat (doubtless for protection!) *under his arm* during the whole journey. Other members of this if somewhat Bohemian certainly hardworking class, relate how among the students was a young man named C——r, of French extraction, but of no very salient talent or qualification. Between this young man and Oliver there seems to have existed something of an antipathy or antagonism, which frequently vented itself in wordy warfare. One night, C——r, palpably alluding to Oliver, said, 'One seldom finds that the sons of great men become great.' 'And you will find out,' retorted Oliver, 'that the sons of little men generally turn out still smaller,' at which there was much applause, as Monsieur C——r was as unpopular as Oliver was popular.

But there are remembrances of the youngest comrade, as was young Madox Brown, of a deeper and more characteristic nature. On one occasion, Monsieur Barthe offered as a prize a month's study gratis for the best drawing executed during the week. One of the students, of a shrewd and energetic mind, suggested that the competitive drawings for this veritable *prix d'honneur* should be submitted to Mr. G. F. Watts, the Royal Academician, and his decision requested. Mr. Watts was duly consulted, and awarded the prize to Oliver, in adjudicating it pointing out how carefully the feet of the figure—that of a boy sitting with one of his feet lifted up and resting on the opposite leg—were drawn, although the boy's head was left unfinished. 'These,' said Mr. Watts, referring to the feet, 'are what students chiefly neglect: everyone can do the head.' Most of his fellow-competitors, it should be pointed out, were double the age of Oliver, who at the time of the competition was only fifteen.

One circumstance which would seem to have made a great impression on the students at Monsieur Barthe's *atélier*, was that of an elderly Frenchwoman persisting for some time in attending the class in order to sketch from the nude. Against this the young Englishmen rebelled, it being contrary to their insular experience for the sexes in such circumstances to work together, although not unusual abroad. Being unable to get rid of their unwished-for companion in any other way, the students threatened to leave in a body unless she left, whereupon the persevering *artiste* was compelled to leave, protesting to the last against not being allowed to finish the month out.

The last and most important result of Oliver's

artistic studies was a water-colour scene from *Silas Marner*. This painting, now in the possession of his father, was exhibited at the Exhibition of the Society of French Artists, in Bond Street, in 1872, and is described by the editors of his works as the most careful, and, on the whole, much the finest of his artistic productions. 'Old Silas,' they say, in their graphic description of the picture, 'with the little girl Eppie tucked under his arm, and a lantern in his hand, is shown finding the body of Godfrey Cass's wife lying on the thickly snow-strewn ground. The small foot-marks and finger-marks, indicating where the infant had crawled away from her dead mother, are seen leading off to the firelit window and open door of the recluse's cottage. The mingled look of kindliness and miserly distrust on the features, and short-sighted spectacled eyes of Silas, on which the lantern-light glares and flickers, have a strange, half-weird impress of truth, contrasted with the distress on the foundling's face — a distress chiefly selfish, as infantile sorrow must be. The posture of the mother is beautiful; and the whole aspect of the composition startling and mournful, but without being either cold in colour or repellant in sentiment. It may be added that this painting does not, in any one point, recall the style of the elder painter : that is to say, there is nothing of a kind imitative or reproductive either of the father's colour or of his style of drawing or handling ; while at the same time it is true—and not less fortunate than true—that those qualities of prompt, solid, and realistic invention, and of dramatic force and directness in story-telling, which are so markedly distinctive in the parent's pictorial work, reappeared as a genuine and personal inheritance in that of the son.'

Although it must not be taken for granted that during any portion of his life Oliver had quite abandoned his artistic aspirations and labours, with the production of this painting, so highly but deservedly praised, our hero's artistic career may be said to have fittingly terminated. After its completion he may have occasionally dallied with his brush, but the scene from *Silas Marner* was the last picture exhibited by Oliver Madox Brown. Nevertheless, artistic aspirations still haunted his mind, and even on his deathbed he spoke of giving up writing, at least for a time, and of going into the country to paint; and in *Dismal Jemmy*, apparently one of the latest productions of his pen, he feelingly alludes to the hopes and aspirations of 'that thrilling period of professional life in which the young landscape-painter's excited imagination pictures his whole future life and happiness as trembling on the jealous lips of the Suffolk Street hanging committee.' 'What artist is there,' he asks, 'who does not remember how his heart sank, and how his face grew pale, as he inquired—striving hard all the while to maintain an aspect of indifference—after the fate of his beloved picture?—the first one, may be, which he has dared to consider good enough to submit for its chance of exhibition beside the works of older and of better men. What great painter is there living now,' adds Oliver, 'who does not recollect the wild vicissitudes of his early career?—its sacred unutterable delights; and, above all, its profound heart-rending sorrows. Bygone pleasure turns sour in the remembrance of an old man,' is the lad's shrewd comment, 'but how unutterably sweet those ancient sorrows seem to him!—how he longs to face them again, if only it were possible!'

At the house of his parents in Fitzroy Square Oliver mixed with many of the *élite* of London literary and artistic society. At all times the abode of the Madox Browns has been a favourite *rendezvous* for men and women of genius, but especially during 1870 and the two succeeding years were their 'At Homes' attended by throngs of representative people, sure of a cordial reception from their host and hostess and their daughters (now Mrs. Rossetti and Mrs. Hueffer). Poets and painters, authors and critics, sculptors and musicians, and the leading members of many professions, met at frequent intervals in those hospitable rooms in order to see and be seen, to hear and be heard, and to interchange those sparkling scintillations of wit and wisdom which are thrown off when genius encounters genius. In this attractive society Oliver was quite at home, his youth being lost sight of in the charm of his brilliant conversation and the solidity of his judgment. Already he had been an extensive reader, having either in their original languages, or through the medium of translation, made himself acquainted with the masterpieces of European literature. Naturally the *Belles Lettres* had the greatest attraction for him, those of France and England supplying his chief mental pabulum. Among the ancient classics Lucretius was his favourite, and never failed to arouse his interest.

Conversant with literature, son of a famous artist, and, apparently, already on the high-road to artistic reputation, Oliver was universally welcomed by his parents' guests as an associate well worth knowing. He was accustomed to say himself, that from childhood he had been surrounded by men of genius, and when he was still a child, men whose names are 'household words,' but whom to particularize would be needless, were wont to bring him playthings, and joining with him in childlike sport, in order to amuse him would break the toys before they went away. One of the fortunate privileges which Oliver enjoyed was, in the character of pupil, to be closely associated with Monsieur Jules Andrieu during a considerable portion of the years 1870 to 1874. M. Andrieu, now French Consul at Jersey, being then resident in London, undertook to instruct Oliver in French and Latin. A first-rate 'humanist,' as his countrymen would say, Monsieur Andrieu was something more than a mere teacher of languages: at the time when political troubles forced him to abandon the career he was making for himself in Paris, he was already favourably known as a writer, having by several works, and notably by his small French History, evinced his learning and capacity.

What Oliver obtained from M. Andrieu were more frequently the brilliant outpourings of a full mind, or epigrammatic discourse on all conceivable literary topics, rather than arid disquisitions on the technical difficulties of a foreign tongue. Occasionally, however, the time was entirely devoted to the theme proposed for the day, Lucretius being the author generally selected; and the pupil must have been dull indeed who did not benefit by the ready reply and apt illustration with which M. Andrieu was at all times prepared. It will readily be comprehended what a deep impression his tutor's intellectual tastes and literary proclivities would produce upon a youth of Oliver's impressibility, and it is by no means impossible that the lad's earliest efforts in the direction of prose literature were, to some extent, albeit unconsciously, instigated by M. Andrieu's precept and practice. Yet Oliver was, to all appearance, a very idle lad, and his tutor being a great scholar himself, was naturally anxious to see his pupil learn: probably, notwithstanding all his wit and imagination, he was not quite acute enough to comprehend exactly what the boy was about. One day, therefore, he took occasion to speak sharply to him, writing to him soon afterwards, however, to express the hope that he had not hurt his feelings. Oliver replied, in the only letter of his M. Andrieu has preserved, with a warm declaration of friendship and esteem, feelings which no subsequent events served to alienate.

Among the less important incidents of 1872, the year which ushered in the most remarkable event in Oliver's career, was a pedestrian tour which he commenced, but never completed, through Kent and Sussex. A friend had made out for him a route that should lead through several of the most interesting places in these counties, and Oliver, with his usual sturdy independence started off alone, about the beginning of September. On the 10th of the month he wrote home from Edenbridge: 'I am going to-day as far as East Grinstead. I passed through Chiddingstone yesterday — such a wonderful old village. The newest house was built in 1691. The inns are very cheap. I have not spent much as yet. I have seen some fine landscapes, but wish it was not so tiring to walk through (them).'

It will readily be understood, however, that a youth of Oliver's temperament, loving London, and accustomed to that brilliant life which only appears to arouse itself towards night-tide, would speedily mope and grow weary of the long, dull September evenings spent in solitude, or in the, to him, uninteresting society which is met with in the parlours of country inns. The youth's imagination might be impressed by the associations connected with the time-honoured ancestral homes he visited, and his artistic eye delighted with the natural beauties he beheld, but his delicate physique rebelled against the unwonted exercise he had to endure, whilst the solitariness of his journey must have been extremely oppressive to one so accustomed to brilliant conversation and intellectual intercourse as he was. He soon wearied of his journey, and about the third or fourth day after he had left town he returned home unexpectedly, with his feet much chafed by the unaccustomed amount of country walking undergone. All these minor troubles, had they been shared with a genial companion, would have been regarded as amusing trifles to be laughed at; the mistake was, the having undertaken such a journey alone, especially in the shortening, saddening September days.

Although Oliver greatly admired the scenery along some portions of his route, and during his last illness spoke of revisiting East Grinstead when better, in order to paint a view of it, he did not much enjoy his solitary walk. Among other matters, he complained of the difficulty of getting things fit to eat. One day, arriving about noon at a small roadside inn, he insisted upon being provided with a regular dinner, and whilst it was being cooked (it consisted of chicken, bacon, and beans out of the adjacent garden, and was pronounced by him to have been 'very nice'), Oliver discovered an old book, a kind of antiquated 'Joe Miller's' collection, in which he found various quaint anecdotes that he afterwards related at home with the fresh and fantastic exaggeration he so delighted in. One story in the ancient tome he was accustomed to repeat with great gusto, was something to this effect :

Once upon a time there was a deeply pious old lady living in some secluded village. A swindler, getting acquainted with her credulity, contrived to introduce himself to her, and even succeeded in persuading her that he was an angelic being in disguise, sent on a mission from heaven. A detective tracked the rascal to his retreat, and soon made himself cognizant of his little game. Desirous of getting the fellow away without much fuss, he informed the good old lady upon whom the rogue was preying that he himself was St. Peter, the custodian of the gates of heaven, and that this particular angel had left without permission, and that he had been sent to bring him back. Upon hearing this, the saintly dame, who had probably been already heavily mulcted by her celestial guest, joyfully assented to his immediate removal.

In this recital we have only been enabled to recover the barest outline of the original story, and are not quite certain even of the order in which the characters stood to each other in the hierarchy, but in Oliver's bright, keen, but playful repetition of the anecdote, it may be well assumed that not a single point was lost sight of or slurred over.

Beyond his recollections of the old jest-book, the young artist does not seem to have had much to relate of his short tour. One incident, however, that he related with characteristic animation, was of meeting with a party of drunken sailors, who favoured him with a volley of abuse because he would not, or could not, tell them the name of some wild plant by the roadside. 'What was the use of his being a landsman,' they shouted, 'if he could not even tell them the name of a plant when they came on shore?'

# THE BLACK SWAN.

## O. M. B.

### DIED NOVEMBER, 1874.

As one who strives from some fast steamer's side
   To note amid the backward-spinning foam
   And keep in view some separate wreath therefrom,
That cheats him even the while he views it glide
(Merging in other foam-tracks stretching wide),
   So strive we to keep clear that day our home
   First saw you riven—a memory thence to roam,
A shattered blossom on the eternal tide!

Oh, broken promises that showed so fair!
Oh, morning sun of wit set in despair!
   Oh, brows made smooth as with the Muses' chrism!
   Oh, Oliver! ourselves Death's cataclysm
Must soon o'ertake—but not in vain—not where
   Some vestige of your thought outspans the abysm!

                                               F. M. B.

*April*, 1883.

## CHAPTER III.

### THE BLACK SWAN.

'Rara avis in terris.'
OVID.

THUS far it has not been possible to advert to much in the life of Oliver Madox Brown that might not be paralleled in the lives of many other youths. Following in the footsteps of his father, an artist of first-class reputation, he had instinctively taken to brush and palette, and although he had already displayed considerable talent in the hereditary art, neither relative nor friend could express much more than satisfaction at the not very unusual circumstance of a son following fairly well in the path a parent had marked out so clearly. It is true that whilst little more than a child in years the boy had produced some few sonnets which had excited pleasing hopes—hopes, however, a lengthy period of silence and apparent distaste for literary honours had long since quelled.

An important crisis was about to occur in Oliver's life: a startling change that was to open out a brilliant vista of attractive labour and anticipated fame, and that was for the future and for ever to clear him from any further suspicion of wilful idleness. Left, perhaps, somewhat unhopefully, to follow out his own impulses, the youth, all unknown even to his nearest relatives, had been carefully and artistically creating a literary *chef d'œuvre*. During the cold winter of 1871-2, closeted in his own room, and without even the comfort of a fire, Oliver had been writing one of those imperishable works, so few, so far between, which once read imprint the reader's memory as with uneffaceable runes. He had been writing *The Black Swan*, 'the most remarkable prose story,' as his editors truly assert, 'ever penned by a youth not older than from sixteen to seventeen.' Precocious as this story was in execution, in inception it was even more so, for we are informed that its author had first 'thought out his narrative when fifteen years of age, and had at that time projected writing it in verse, a scheme from which, independent and tenacious of his own personality in all things, he was diverted by reflecting that, among the authors belonging to, or highly prized in, his own social circle, there were various writers of poetry, but few or none who produced prose fiction.' Such a reflection, and such a determination in a youth of Oliver's age, are in themselves strong evidence of his originality and courage.

When the young author had completed some few chapters of his story he handed them to his sister Lucy to read, and by Miss Madox Brown (now Mrs. Rossetti) the manuscript was taken to her father, in what may readily be believed to have been an ecstasy of delight. The surprise and pleasure of Mr. Madox Brown at this new and unanticipated evidence of his son's genius were so great, that it was some days, we are informed, 'before he could calmly realize the fact.' Encouraged by such a sympathetic audience, 'fit but few,' Oliver worked at his romance with all the energy of youth and hope, and in a comparatively short time had completed it. Happily, the wisdom of his editors has caused them to preserve and publish the story of *The Black Swan* in its original and unweakened form. The story, even when stripped of its artistic accessories and denuded of that glamour genius has enveloped it in, is sufficiently terrible.

Told in our plain prose, the narrative is that a certain Gabriel Denver, an Australian colonist of mixed English and Portuguese parentage, has to embark for England in order to make good his claim to a considerable legacy to which he has become entitled. He is a married man, his union, however, having been more one of convenience than of affection. Dorothy possessed a sufficient sum of money to free Denver from the embarrassments ill-judged speculations had cast him into, and being of his own age, evidently enamoured of him, and the most, if not only, suitable *parti* available, he had married her. If Denver had ever fancied he loved Dorothy, he soon forgot the feeling, and as she was utterly undemonstrative in response to the fire and passion of his semi-southern temperament, he speedily became indifferent and she callous. Of course, he could not leave his wife alone in Australia, and so, on a certain day in December, 1824, he left home in order to secure a passage for himself and Dorothy in *The Black Swan*, an emigrant vessel just returning to England.

No one but a writer thoroughly intimate with ships and ship-life could have so technically discussed the merits of *The Black Swan* and its surroundings, but into those technicalities there is no necessity to enter here ; it suffices, therefore, to say, that on board this vessel Denver beheld, and utterly oblivious of his marriage vow, at first sight loved, a young girl just verging on womanhood, and who, accompanied by an old servant, was likewise bound for England. On this first occasion the passionate-hearted colonist, as he rowed round the ship, beheld Laura Conway for an instant only, as with bare arms and lightly covered shoulders she leant on the sill of a cabin casement, but in that instant he lived a lifetime. With a fidelity to nature, that it seems impossible could have been gathered at second-hand, and with a natural fidelity a more experienced *raconteur* would scarcely have dared to express, the young author writes:

'Laura's beautiful eyes had ensnared his soul with their magnetism, though *he could hardly remember their colour;* still less really distinctly the shape of her face. An indistinct impression of sun-sparkling, wind-blown hair, of her bare arms and white shoulders, was all that was left for his imagination to fill up and complete.'— 'There is always in the human heart,' Oliver adds to this psychological sketch, 'no matter how bad, or dull, or callous it may be in other directions, a certain store of conjugal love which can never be wasted by any but legitimate use, however long it may lie unused.'

Now, and for the first time in his life, Denver really loved. His wife passed out of his mind, 'and all the rest of the day as he paced about looking on the ship, a divine ecstasy of yearning seemed to have fallen on him. . . . . It seemed strange that all that time he should have shrunk from going on board the ship where she (Laura) was, until the last moment.' 'I think,' is one out of the many psychologically true remarks of Oliver, ' it was a kind of anticipation of delight, a prolongation of longing to its uttermost limits of desire, which kept him on shore till his wife arrived.'

Denver and his wife embarked at night, and ' before morn the signal-lamps of *The Black Swan* had passed into the gloom over the horizon.' The ship sped on her way, and after some time one of the four passengers, the old servant, died, and Laura was left alone in the world. But Denver loved her blindly, passionately, madly, in such a way as only those who love hopelessly can love, for it seems as if it were almost impossible, so hapless is unfortunate humanity, for any real love to be lawful or sanctioned by law. The guileless Laura could not help feeling and reciprocating Denver's affection, although she knew he was married, and had daily to see his wife, now the only other female on board. Dorothy, also, knew of her husband's love for their fellow-passenger, and that she herself had become utterly distasteful in his sight, so her hatred for them both grew deep, intense, and none the less dangerous that the embers of her wrath smouldered awhile. What subtle insight into the mental workings of these folk is expressed by their delineator, and how skilfully he poses them before us, let these words prove:

'Her mind, scarcely developed yet, was innocent as a child's, with the same flow of passionate feelings in its unsounded and unsuspected depths. . . . . Unsuspected, because as yet no particular aspect of thought or passion was stamped on her face, despite a certain dreamy look, which at times seemed as though it might yet develop, at a touch, into something more defined in character; and this united, perhaps, with that strange, fitful energy, under which, when resisted, the weakest woman sometimes grows terrible, and which all women, moreover, are capable of.'

'The commencement and extremes of human passion are dumb, and in speech well nigh expressionless; only the soul comprehends what the tongue fails to articulate—the first promptings of love. Notwithstanding that Denver and Laura were together all the day, save for the sullen unseen presence of the wife, yet I think that his heart and will would have failed him had he attempted to say in *words* what he *knew* they were thinking of, for a secret instinct told him that she was beginning to love him. Now, to love and be loved was become a new principle in this man's life; before this vague unexplored something all else seemed to dwindle and die away. His life seemed turned into a trance, like an opium-eater's, and when dragged from it, he could have turned fiercely on his disturber, only to sink back into its unrealized depths with redoubled longing. At first, his wife, Dorothy, seemed a mere shadow to him, a relic of his former life; but as this antagonism between her and Laura deepened and developed, and the future began to loom up before him, he saw what step he had taken, and apathy turned into dislike and defiance, and then again into fierce smouldering hatred, as he felt the ties which bound him to this woman, unable as he was ever to avoid her presence in the ship.'

Confined in the narrow limits of a sailing vessel, it was impossible for these three persons, each one filled with surging passions, to live long together without their feelings finding some means of disclosure. The hour arrived, and the opportunity came. An accidental meeting of Denver and Laura in the dusky twilight afforded occasion for a verbal revelation of what both had long silently felt. With passionate impetuosity Denver poured forth his long pent-up feelings, and Laura confessed that she loved him.

Their words fell in a third person's hearing. Hidden in the shadow, the neglected wife heard the confession, and saw the caresses of the lovers; but conquering her first impulse of interrupting them, she turned and passed noiselessly along the deck and down into the cabin. Both Laura and Denver had seen a female 'figure emerge from the black mass made by the boat against the luminous sky, and appear with startling distinctness in the moonlight, which streamed by on both sides,' and both knew that it was the discarded wife. ' A dark foreboding filled Laura's mind. During that short half-hour Dorothy's very existence had been driven out of her head; but now, brought so unexpectedly to her view, she must have foreseen for a moment something of what must follow, sooner or later, shut up for months in the loneliness of the ship as they were. But it was no use thinking; she had given her love irrecoverably to Denver.

' Henceforth he must exist as a part of her being—it seemed to her that she could not live without him—she trusted blindly in him, and it made her shudder as she thought that Dorothy's claim over Denver might necessitate their separation. . . . God had made them for each other, and was *she* to part them ? . . . Could she have really supposed Dorothy capable of holding them apart, she would have turned on her with fierce unrelenting resistance; but, as it was, cast off from them and utterly helpless as she seemed, it was impossible to hate her: rather never think of her at all.'

Therefore, the lovers both, 'as by some common dread, avoided mentioning Dorothy: her name never once passed their lips from the first time they had spoken together.' After the first interchange of passionate declaration between the two lovers, 'each day seemed like the past one'; and whilst Denver 'grew more infatuated with Laura, and more morbid when she was out of sight, as he thought of the heaven which would surround him but for the presence and existence of the brooding revengeful woman his wife,' that injured wife kept silently to herself, meditating over a terrible, an unparalleled act of vengeance. So bitter was it at times for the wretched husband to endure the presence of the still more wretched wife, that he could hardly refrain from expressing his fierce hatred of her whenever she came near him, whilst he knew but too truly, 'from her strange silence and behaviour, that some act of her resentment would occur before long.'

With this ill-assorted company on board, the vessel continued to beat up against contrary winds until within five days' sail of the Cape. Becalmed one night, *The Black Swan* lay almost motionless on the waters. Save two, kept sleepless by their passions, all on board her were asleep: even the helmsman at the wheel was slumbering over it. The two were Dorothy (who had overheard Laura promise to meet Denver on deck after nightfall, and in a fit of the mad jealousy she could no longer restrain had determined to interrupt them), and Denver, who paced the deck in wild impatience.

After a weary waiting, he beheld the outline of a woman's form; he went to her impetuously, and clasping her to his breast, whispered in a low, almost trembling voice, words of passionate love. 'Then, as he seemed to kiss her face, a sudden tremor stopped his words, and the woman broke away from his embrace with an angry exclamation, while he, starting back from her, appeared to stagger for an instant as if a snake had stung him. . . . The woman whom he had embraced so passionately began crying out in an exasperated voice:

'" So I've found you out at last, Denver!

How dare you treat me in this fashion? I'm *not Laura*, I'm your own lawful wife. . . . Ah! you sneak back soon enough now, but you shan't escape me! We two are alone at last. You shall give me an account of your conduct and the way you keep the oath you swore to at God's altar."

'"Damn you, will you never let me have one moment to myself, without poisoning it with your presence? It's bad enough to have to *think* about you," the man answered fiercely.

'"You're a liar!" she interrupted in a passionate, screaming voice. "I've neither been near you nor spoken to you for six weeks. Good God, what gratitude! I've toiled my life out for you, to sit silently by myself in this dreary, stifling ship, neglected by everyone, watching you make love to another woman, before my very face, hour after hour, day after day, week after week, till it's driven me mad!"'

And with similar reproaches and invectives the wretched woman poured forth the history of her wrongs, and screamed forth her threats of vengeance, until finally, 'her throat seemed quite exhausted with passion, and she broke down into a violent fit of hysterical sobbing.' As Denver moved away she followed him, renewing her passionate screaming and maddening reproaches, until at last, exasperated beyond human control by some threatening words he let fall, she dared him to fling her overboard and add murder to his misdeeds. For the moment, stung to desperation by her words, he almost appeared ready to yield to her suggestion, when suddenly a woman's clear, sweet voice rose through the night-air, but a few yards from where they stood, singing :

'" Alas! who knows or cares, my love,
　　　If our love live or die—
　If thou thy frailty, sweet, should'st prove,
　　　Or my soul thine deny ?
　Yet merging sorrow in delight,
　Love's dream disputes our devious night.

'" None know, sweet love, nor care a thought
　　　For our hearts' vague desire,
　Nor if our longing come to nought,
　　　Or burn in aimless fire ;
　Let them alone, we'll waste no sighs :
　Cling closer, love, and close thine eyes !"'

The effect of Laura's song, for it was hers, was as magical on her two hearers as was that of Pippa on Ottima and Sebald: the maddened wife slunk away into the darkness, and the desperate man forgot his anger in his despair. He leant over the bulwarks, his heart beating wildly as he thought of what might have happened. ' Never could such a deed as his reckless, maddened temper so narrowly escaped burdening him with, have seemed more degrading and cowardly, and antagonistic to any human being than the past few moments now seemed to Denver. He had, it is true, more than once been unable to restrain the drift of his speculations, yet it had seemed to him that what he had thought of was only a remote *impossible* possibility, something *he* could *never* come to. Now this ordeal he had passed through was a proof of his reckless temper and moral weakness such as made the strong man shudder and shudder again as he thought of what he had escaped from, and what a few more days or even hours might still bring him to.'

Denver's reflections were suddenly put a stop to by the terrible discovery that the ship, *The Black Swan*, was on fire! 'No one,' says our author, 'who has not witnessed the effects of such an alarm as this can comprehend the horror of it, or realize the sensations of those who, failing to baffle the flames, see nothing before them, as they retreat foot by foot, but a choice between two deaths, *fire* or *water;* their home a burning furnace, floating, tossed about, on the immense sea. The two elements most utterly opposed to each other, combined for the destruction—the pitiless annihilation—of the common enemy, man.'

It is not our purpose to dilate upon the fearful scenes which followed the discovery of the fire: it suffices to state that the final result of this calamity was that all on board, save three, perished in the flames, and that those three, by the cruel irony of fate, were Laura, Denver, and Dorothy. These three human beings, through a series of events that appear neither improbable nor unnatural, alone escaped from the burning ship, and for four days, without food and without water, were tossed about helplessly in an open boat on the illimitable, pathless ocean. The horrors of those four days were enough to break down the strongest. Dorothy, if she were not mad before became so now, and having drunk of sea-water to quench her thirst, died raving, in her delirium confessing, what an acute reader of the romance may have already guessed, that it was she who had fired the ship.

At the expiration of the four days the two survivors were picked up by a passing vessel; but the exposure and privation had been too much for Laura's delicate frame: she died on board the ship that had rescued them, and thus far Dorothy was avenged. But the tragedy was not yet ended. Night came, and the crew were discussing the burial of the dead girl, when they were startled by seeing above the dark outline of the bulwark, near the helm, 'a strange, black *silhouette* appear and pause for a moment—a man carrying a dead woman. Her head and neck hangs back passively, and long hair, bright with the moonlight, streams from it in the wind, while her hands fall dangling helplessly—this is all seen plainly against the sky; the next instant it is gone.'

Denver, for it was he, was seen to press one passionate kiss upon the inanimate form, and then, in his delirium, leap with it into the sea. And thus poetic justice was satisfied!

This is the barest possible outline, and a naturally common-place aspect, of Oliver Madox Brown's wonderful story—a story which had to be so manipulated and mangled before it could be transformed into *Gabriel Denver*, that, in its new plumage, *The Black Swan* is scarcely recognisable. But even in its reconstructed form, much was left to call forth the admiration of the critics—although they were ignorant in many instances of the author's youth. The elaborate knowledge of nautical affairs, and the fidelity with which the various aspects of the open ocean are described, are quite marvellous when it is remembered that their delineator had never been out of sight of the English coasts; yet still more surprising is it to find a boy with such deep insight into abnormal, but not utterly unknown, traits of humanity as he displays. Much that he describes *can* only have been given from personal experience, but rarely, if ever before, has a lad of seventeen been known to have been endowed with such knowledge. Passing by without allusion some of the more complicated physiological emotions described, let us regard such mental problems as are referred to in the following words, and then endeavour to gauge their author's precocity:

'To die—to cease to exist—to look at his arm, still with its old useless strength in it, and feel that in a while he would be without power over its movements; to use his vision, but think that in a while his eyes would darken till they could no longer see Laura's face, that his ear would no longer hear her voice, that voice which once thrilled through his own soul;—to live still, and yet know that his senses were beginning to ebb like a sinking tide, or to dissolve like a pool of water sucked up by the power of the sun. To lie as if paralyzed in helpless contemplation of the future unlived days, the warmth and effulgency of which shone so brightly in front of him, while the present slowly darkened and vanished around him, as the last sobs of his life —breath exhaled into the dreary blank nonexistent nothingness which men call death—leaving the life before him so miserably *un*lived;—it made him like some thirst-maddened animal tantalized by a transitory desert mirage. It was too terribly incredible.'

Still more strangely mature are some of this lad's references to sleep and dreams, as when, for instance, he alludes to the 'sudden burst of terror, such as all men feel on awakening from the slumber they have begun at night, with hearts over-confident for the morrow's trouble. I think,' is his reflection, 'an awakened sleeper always sees his last thoughts in a kind of inversion.' Also, among other unyouthful expressions of thought may be noted his continual *suggestion* all through this romance of the insignificance of a human being as compared with the immensity of nature, and how, all-regardless of his wishes, wants, or woes, the great work of the universe goes on slowly, surely, and irresistibly changeless, despite all the impotent efforts of man to change or even to guide it.

Appealing more strongly, however, to the feelings of the general reader, will be the magnificent description of the ship on fire. The ghastly scenes which occur during the burning of *The Black Swan* are not only painted with the minute fidelity of a Defoe, or an Edgar Poe, but described with all the graphic *vraisemblance* of a personal spectator. However unsympathetic a reader the peruser of the work may be, it will be as impossible for him to escape being fascinated by the grand picture of the fire as it was for the unfortunate albatross to escape from the vivid attraction of the flames themselves.

After the wonderfully realistic account of the conflagration, these thoroughly characteristic expressions are invoked: 'There is, perhaps, nothing in nature more strange to reflect on, than this magic transmutation by fire which we witness daily with so little thought or comment. To see a substantial object take light and vanish away in flame before our very eyes, not dying invisibly, as our souls or lives do, but simply vanishing from sight, while only an utterly disproportionate sediment of its ashes remains behind, is miraculous.'

It may safely be averred that, take it for all in all, it will be difficult in the whole range of English literature to discover a more terribly dramatic, or more weirdly picturesque tableau, than that of those three strangely-brought-together human beings, Laura, Denver, and Dorothy, tossed about in that frail, oarless boat, on the angry, hungry ocean. However puny the passions of these powerless creatures may appear in comparison with the stupendous sublimity of the eternal ocean they drift upon, it is they, tiny specks on the face of nature though they be, who kindle our hearts to pity or contemn: their awful environments scarcely invoke a shudder whilst their all-absorbing fate still trembles in the balance. Till the tragedy is complete by the death of the last actor, the terrific magnificence of their *entourage* scarcely attracts the admiration of the awe-stricken spectator; but when that spell is broken by the disappearance of the last victim of the fated trio, we are enabled to award due meed of praise to the wonderfully realistic scenery by which the *dramatis personæ* are surrounded.

*GABRIEL DENVER.*

**Prefixed to the first Manuscript of his Earliest Literary Offspring was this Sonnet.**

---

No more these passion-worn faces shall men's eyes
   Behold in life.  Death leaves no trace behind
   Of their wild hate and wilder love, grown blind
In desperate longing, more than the foam which lies
Splashed up awhile where the showered spray descries
   The waves whereto their cold limbs were resigned;
   Yet ever doth the sea-wind's undefined
Vague wailing shudder with their dying sighs.
For all men's souls 'twixt sorrow and love are cast
   As on the earth each lingers his brief space,
   While surely nightfall comes where each man's face
In death's obliteration sinks at last
   As a deserted wind-tossed sea's foam-trace—
Life's chilled boughs emptied by death's autumn blast.
                           OLIVER MADOX BROWN.

## CHAPTER IV.

### *GABRIEL DENVER.*

TO comprehend the enormous chasm which gapes between genius and the conventional, it is only necessary to contrast *The Black Swan* in its original condition with the white-washed foundling, *Gabriel Denver*, commercial prudence bargained for. In the terrible narrative as conceived and as executed by its author, the three important personages of the tragedy are beheld from the first struggling as helplessly as the characters of a Greek drama against their cruel, irresistible fate. For Laura, Gabriel, and Dorothy, the final catastrophe was unavoidable, whilst the string upon which these puppets of circumstance were strung was the hapless marriage-cord by which Gabriel was bound to Dorothy. Yet to satisfy the supposed prudery of a temporary public, this *raison d'être* of the story had to be sacrificed, and the outraged wife transformed into a spiteful cousin, whilst the stern poetic justice which so unerringly overtook the couple who loved not wisely, had, to please the enervated palate of circulating-library-subscribers, to be harlequinaded into the stock nostrum of bridal favours, beautiful progeny, and 'they lived happily ever afterwards!' Oh, what a fall was there from the weird and appropriate end of the tragedy! How it wrung young Oliver's heart to mutilate his first-born thus may never be revealed, but some glimpses of his grief will be gained by those who read his correspondence on the subject.

However, the throes of literary labour are fruitless without the intervention of a publisher, and a publisher had to be found ere *The Black Swan* could be ushered into the world of letters. Probably the search was not a prolonged one in Oliver's case; at any rate, there does not seem to be any reason for concealing the interesting fact that it was due to female intervention that the romance ultimately found its way into the hands of Messrs. Smith, Elder and Co. The late Mrs. Lomes Dickinson, wife of the artist, and daughter of Mr. W. Smith Williams, having had an opportunity of reading the story in manuscript, was so greatly struck by its power and originality that she did all she could to interest her father in it. He read it, and that he was highly impressed by it his acts and words will show. He wrote to the young author, criticizing certain things in the work in a friendly way, but requesting him to offer it to Messrs. Smith, Elder and Co., for publication. Oliver's reply, dated 27th September, 1872, was in a very different tone to the confident one generally adopted by juvenile authors:

'I trust you will excuse my delay in not having answered your kind and encouraging letter before this, but I have been for the last week so ill that at first I was scarcely able even to read it. With regard to submitting my novel to Messrs. Smith and Elder, I hardly know what to say. If you consider it worth while I should certainly have no objection to offering it for publication—if on the contrary you were to think it has positively no chance of being accepted, I should prefer not to offer it: in fact, I would trust implicitly to whatever you yourself may think best on the subject. I have not the slightest objection to modifying the harshness of the plot so far as I am able, for I perfectly recognise the truth and usefulness of the alterations you have so kindly suggested. However, I do not see how I could make Dorothy merely

Denver's cousin and not his wife. The only excuse that can be offered for Denver's conduct seems to me to be the utterly isolated situation he is placed in, and the extreme and unexpected suddenness of his passion. He, undoubtedly, behaves badly, and the tragic ending he comes to is supposed to be a just retaliation upon him. The passage you mention in Chap. VIII. I will remove—I had, indeed, intended to alter it from the first. I have been for more than three months engaged on a second work—a story of Dartmoor and Devonshire country life, and have in consequence had no time to make many of the alterations I have intended in the MS. of *Gabriel Denver*. I cannot think how I can have made such a blunder as to forget the gold that was in the boat—for I certainly thought of what the sailors would do with it, when I first described its falling out of the man's pocket. The first chapter will have to be considerably remodelled. . . . If you do not think *Gabriel Denver* fit to be shown to Messrs. Smith and Elder, would you kindly allow me, in a short while, to submit to you the first four or five chapters of my new story? With many thanks for the encouragement your kind and long letter has given me,

   Believe me, dear sir,
    Very faithfully yours,
     OLIVER MADOX BROWN.'

The reply of Mr. Smith Williams was so encouraging that Oliver felt not only persuaded to offer his romance to that gentleman's firm, but also to endeavour to remodel it in accordance with his suggestions, little as they agreed with his own more artistic views. This, however, it must be confessed, not until much correspondence and some interviews had taken place, and, doubtless, not without a severe mental struggle. In one letter he writes, 'Of course, in the case of my making any very material alterations in the MS. of *Gabriel Denver*,' for so the story was to be renamed, 'I shall be only too glad to avail myself of the many valuable suggestions you were kind enough to offer me after reading it. In fact, I should completely rewrite the whole story page by page. It is scarcely ten months since I have written it; but there are, nevertheless, a good many things in it which, now, I should not care to publish as my own.' In the following month, January, 1873, he writes to his younger sister: 'Although I have, at last, come to an understanding with my publisher with respect to *Gabriel Denver*, some time will still elapse (owing to certain alterations I have consented very unwillingly to make) before its final publication.'

On the 17th of January he wrote to Mr.

Smith Williams: 'Would you care to look at the first three chapters of *Gabriel Denver*? I have rewritten them, and one is quite new. . . . I should at any rate like you to look at the opening chapter, as I think you particularly mentioned it to me.' The rewritten chapters were looked at, and further objections raised as to their suitability, especially with respect to the position of one which Oliver desired to commence the work with, justly deeming, from a truly artistic point of view, that the introductory pages should be of a highly attractive nature, whilst Mr. Smith Williams objected, on almost equally tenable grounds, that they should not be retrospective or anticipatory, which they were. Of course, Oliver had to give way, relinquishing one point after another, until, finally, he was driven out of his very last entrenchment. Writing to Mr. Smith Williams on the 24th of January, he says:

'MY DEAR SIR,

I am sorry to differ from you in opinion respecting the chapter that ought to stand first —the more so, when I think of the very large experience you must have had in dealing with novels; but I cannot help feeling that it would considerably damp the reader's interest in the book, were the opening chapter to be a weak one. I have hitherto considered, that with all model works of art, the impetuousness of the first chapter is a *sine quâ non*.

The Dorothy point I am willing enough to yield, because I fancy your reasons must be extremely just: we might call her *Deborah*. I think on the whole that it would perhaps be best not to give her the same surname as her cousin Denver. I have, therefore, decided upon *Deborah Mallinson*, as the name most suited to her.

The other point I will, of course, yield also, should you absolutely require it—but it would not be without reluctance on my part.

Could you give me any idea of when you would be able to publish my story, or if there would be any particular season in which it would be desirable to bring it out? I shall scarcely be a month longer over it, and will send you the MS. by about the end of February.

With many thanks for your kindness,
  Believe me, dear sir,
    Very faithfully yours,
      OLIVER MADOX BROWN.'


On the 10th March Oliver writes to Mr. Williams to say that he has completed the story as well as he is able, and trusts that it will now be considered satisfactorily ended : he remarks that he is still prepared to make any other alterations deemed necessary, being, probably, by this time quite ready to turn his black swan into a white goose, or an 'ugly duckling,' or, indeed, prepared to sacrifice it altogether. He points out that chapters i., ix., xviii., xix., and the Conclusion are entirely new, and that certain other changes have been made in the work.

At last the publisher's literary adviser was satisfied, whatever the author may have been, and gave an intimation that the story might be used in the *Cornhill Magazine*, which would, of course, have been a very valuable and flattering introduction for so young and unknown an author. On the 13th instant, acknowledging this letter, Oliver writes :

'I am extremely glad to learn that you are pleased with the end of *Gabriel Denver*, as some little time and trouble have been taken in thinking it out and composing it. . . . It is exceedingly kind of you to have submitted the manuscript to the editor of the *Cornhill*. Should Mr. Stephen consider it worthy of acceptance it would be a most unexpected piece of good fortune to such an inexperienced writer as myself.'

The romance was placed in the hands of the *Cornhill* editor, who wrote on the 26th of March offering to make an appointment with its author. On the following day Oliver appears to have called on Mr. Leslie Stephen, but no definite arrangement was come to, and for some weeks the poor lad was kept in a state of uncertainty and suspense. At last a communication was received from Mr. Smith Williams, wherein he states: 'Your story of *Gabriel Denver* has been under consideration of the editor of the *Cornhill Magazine*, who begs me to say he is very sorry that he cannot accept it; but he found it necessary to choose another story, which, for various reasons, was better suited for the magazine. He adds, however, "I am still of opinion that Mr. Brown's story shows much power and promise."' Notwithstanding this editorial modicum of 'faint praise,' the publishers had the justice, after all the pains Oliver had taken to adapt his story to their wishes, to offer what Mr. Williams trusted would be a compensation for Oliver's disappointment, to purchase *Gabriel Denver* for fifty pounds. 'It will make only one volume of the usual novel size,' adds that gentleman, 'and though your name is not yet known to the public as a writer, I hope that your first book will make so strong an impression on the novel readers as to establish your popularity as a writer of romance.'

Thus it was agreed that the work of art which had been so mutilated to please the novel readers should be published by Messrs. Smith, Elder and Co. The usual suggestions took place as to the technicalities of the work's 'get-up,' both as to its inside and outside appearance. On one occasion, Mr. Williams writes to ask for 'some suitable motto to suggest the character of the story, or excite attention, and which would lessen the blank space of the title-page.' Oliver was unable to discover anything English which he cared for, but was enabled to forward the following highly appropriate French motto, suggested or invented by, it is believed, his friend, M. Andrieu: '*Le bonheur vient souvent bien tard—après la mort de toutes nos espérances. Aussi faut-il aux malheureux beaucoup d'esprit pour le reconnaître, et de force pour l'arrêter au passage.*'

The blank space thus happily filled in, the next matter to be considered was the dedication, and on the 16th of July, Oliver is found writing about that and other connected items thus: 'I have just had a sudden idea that I should like to dedicate *Gabriel Denver* to my father, and am desirous to know if you think this would be advisable. I have, certainly, not asked his consent, but I can see no reason why he should object. The only drawback is that I might be thought rather conceited for considering my first work worth dedicating to anybody. Anyhow, I should like very much to do it, if there still remain time.' To this idea of the young author there could not, happily, be any objection; and so he had the proud gratification of seeing his first work inscribed, 'To MY FATHER.'

In the letter quoted from above, Oliver proceeds: 'Thank you for the title-page. As far as I can see, the motto seems to hit off the story well enough. All the proofs are corrected now, so that the volume will be quite ready for publication when the proper season comes round. I don't know if you would care to have any ornament or design made for the binding—if you would, I could easily get them done for you —but I think it might be well to let the cover be as plain as possible.' 'Many thanks for the offer of a design for the cover, which is too good to be neglected,' responded Mr.

Williams, 'as a striking outside might attract notice to a powerful story. If, therefore, you will favour me with a sketch, we will get the binder to engrave it. The only hindrance is Mudie's labels, which interfere with a handsome cover.' Notwithstanding the library labels, a handsome covering was provided for *Gabriel Denver*. At first the young author thought of designing it himself, and wrote to his friend, Mr. Philip B. Marston, 'I am designing a binding for my unfortunate little book, and find it a very difficult and laborious task. There will be a great curling flame very much blown about by the sea-wind, springing and shooting out from the foam of a large wave. It is supposed to be night:—a little light falls on the water beneath and on the clouds above, just dimly outlining them—while two or three stars are visible, and all the rest is hidden in the darkness. Of course, it is purely ornamental and not realistic.'

Oliver, however, relinquished the task of making the desiderated design when he found that his father was willing to undertake it. Accordingly, Mr. Ford Madox Brown made the design himself, and, as will readily be comprehended, a most striking and suggestive one it is. It depicts a ship at sea, on fire, and already partially eaten away by the hungry flames; dense volumes of smoke roll up through the reddened sky, and whirl away into fantastic curls about the book. But the design is treated decoratively rather than pictorially, the burning ship being placed in an emblematic circle, in which the conflagration rages so fiercely that it bursts it, whilst through the attenuated smoke is seen the constellation of the Southern Cross, and the albatross which figures in the story. At the bottom of the cover some large rats, of whose behaviour on the burning ship such suggestive use is made, are seen in characteristic attitudes endeavouring to effect their escape from the ill-fated vessel.

The story was written and rewritten; the design for the cover provided; dedication made and motto selected, and there appeared to be nothing left to do save publish. But another disappointment had to be endured. No wonder if authors are the irritable class the proverbialist would have them be, when the worries, anxieties and annoyances they are subjected to are taken count of. Publishers have an idea that books, like geese, should arrive in flocks, and that the best season for their hatching or addling is a few weeks before Christmas. Poor Oliver's work had to share the common lot, so we find him writing to his father in the summer of 1873, saying, 'I went this morning to call on Mr. Williams about something connected with the printing of *Gabriel Denver*, and he told me that he considered it would be best to put off its publication till October. I suppose he knows what he's about, but it seems to me a great nuisance that the book cannot appear at once.'

However, like Purgatory, everything must come to an end, and so, finally, the long weeks of waiting were over, and on the 5th of November, 1873, *Gabriel Denver* was published. Slowly, but surely, the applause of all those whose approbation Oliver counted worth the winning was gained. Dr. Westland Marston, who had read the proofs of the work, wrote enthusiastically to its young author, 'I really think there is scarcely any crown of fiction which may not eventually be won by a writer who has so begun his career.' Other most gratifying proofs of the profound impression his work had made, and made at once, came to the youth from other valued sources; but what gave him the chiefest and most intense delight was this letter he received from Dante G. Rossetti, for whom he entertained feelings of an almost reverential character:

'Kelmscott, Lechlade,
10 Nov., 1873.

My dear Oliver,

I have read *Gabriel Denver*, and been much astonished and impressed by it. I really believe it must be the most robust literary effort of any imaginative kind that anyone has produced at the age at which you wrote it, and probably even at your present age; though I am uncertain as to the exact time of life at which the Brontë girls wrote their first books. I remember advising you very strongly to make any modifications thought necessary for the circulation of the book; but I fully expected your story to suffer by changes. Still, from what I saw of it in its first form, I think you have managed so well that the strength of the situation is retained, while much is abated of what is unavoidably repelling in it. The position of Deborah must remain a sore in the reader's heart, for all her incendiarism and for all the sympathy the lovers excite.

'The literary quality of the work is surprisingly accomplished and even. However, the last hundred pages or so do not seem to me for the most part quite so finished in execution as the rest. I mean particularly to refer to a certain deliberateness and obviousness of expression—amounting now and then almost to a gossiping tone—which seems to me to be what you have to guard against, but which you have probably fallen into at times (if indeed it strikes others as it does me) by a laudable desire to avoid a flurried tone of sensational narrative. Perhaps I might refer to part of pp. 244—245 as somewhat illustrating what I mean. The description at bottom of 244 seems to require to be more agitated and fitful in its mode of expression for such a moment,—the " beautifully-modelled ankle " seems to me specially *deliberate*. "Most likely Denver expected," etc., seems a little too much from the outside, and the "Stranger than fiction," with which the next paragraph closes, reads almost like intentional bathos.

I hope you will pardon my expressing what I mean in this way, and I do not intend to say that such instances seem to me frequent; but the sustained and almost self-repressed style does appear occasionally to be chargeable with a slight want of infectious electricity, so to speak. But all this is very subordinate and only partially applicable criticism, and the book is undoubtedly quite a wonder. There seems to me no question that you may reach any degree of success in the future, if your interest in your work remains undiminished. Nothing else can influence permanently a man's powers or their due recognition. You are fully armed for the work you are undertaking, and the little song at page 91* shows that you can even write, when called for, verse well able to stand by itself.

With affectionate remembrances,
     Ever yours,
      D. G. ROSSETTI.

P.S.—Cover excellent. Obverse perhaps a *little* Japanese.

P.P.S.—In another edition I would cut out all the *italics*.'

Dante Rossetti's goodness of heart, and the sympathy which he was always ready to accord to any manifestation of talent in youth, were not sufficient in themselves to have prompted him to write in such a laudatory strain: he could not have told his youthful friend that his work was ' the most robust literary effort of any imaginative kind that anyone has produced' at Oliver's age, unless his critical conscience had been fully satisfied that what he said was fact. Oliver, even if he fully recognised his own power, could not fail to ·feel deeply gratified at this prompt and ungrudging acknowledgment of it from such

---

° Beginning, 'Alas! who knows or cares, my love.' *vide* p. 59.

a quarter. On November the 29th he replied to his kind critic:

'DEAR MR. ROSSETTI,

You must really excuse me for having delayed answering your kind letter till now. I thank you most cordially and sincerely for the gratifying and encouraging things you say in it: I only fear you must err far too much on the side of leniency in the very few weaknesses and blemishes you have called my attention to. Your letter surprised and delighted me in more ways than one; for while writing my book, I often thought of you and of what you were likely to say of it, but did not venture to think you would interest yourself so much in it. Certainly I would rather have your approbation for my work—after my father's—than that of any other man living.

I hope you will not mind my having sent your letter on to Messrs. Smith and Elder, but the fact is that Mr. Williams, who took up *Gabriel Denver* first, has been very anxious to know what your opinion would be about it, and I should not have liked to ask you to write to him yourself—although I believe you are acquainted with him.

One review has appeared up to the present

(in the *Academy* for Saturday last), which, upon the whole, is remarkably favourable. . . .
Yours most sincerely,
OLIVER MADOX BROWN.'

On the same day that he wrote the above the elated lad forwarded Dante Rossetti's letter to Messrs. Smith, Elder and Co.'s reader for his perusal. Mr. Williams, in returning the valuable and much valued communication, heartily congratulated Oliver upon such encouraging criticism, adding, 'Mr. Simcox's critique in the *Academy* is appreciative of your powers, and will help the book.'

Before the young author had had time to taste the full bitterness of having written a book, and ere reviews less appreciative than that of Mr. Simcox had had time to appear, in the first flush of authorship Oliver wrote off the following amusing *jeu d'esprit* to his friend, Mr. Philip Bourke Marston:

'*November* 8, 1873.

MY DEAR PHILIP,—

You will be glad to hear my book is out at last.

I have just written an elaborate review thereof, and having copied it out seven times, with a few alterations here and there, I am about to post it to the principal newspapers of the United Kingdom, accompanied by an equal number of Post Office orders (for ten and sixpence each). N.B.—*If you don't insert this, keep the money and write one yourself.* I shall await in great anxiety the result of this new and interesting experiment. . . . . .'

In a letter written to the same friend eighteen days later a different tone had to be adopted: the real 'slings and arrows' of criticism now began to assail the youthful and highly sensitive romancer. 'Have you seen,' he asks, '——'s notice of *Gabriel Denver* in last week's *Athenæum*? I'm told it's of a kind likely to clap a stopper on his circulation for some little time to come. Applied by one novelist to another, " coarse, disagreeable, and hideous," be decidedly sarcastic, if not biting terms. I imagine he read the book through (here and there) and found he didn't like it, so —being highmindedness and respectability personified—he has felt it his duty to say so. As far as I am concerned, anyone may say what he likes about the book, but what I fear is, that Messrs. Smith, Elder and Co. will be for chucking me overboard if *G. D.* don't grow as prosperous as they expected him to; and this prospect is, of course, not by any means the one I am hoping for. However, one mustn't cry out before one's hurt. I'm precious glad his lordship let me off so easy; it's not a fiftieth part so harsh as the lathering . . . had in the same paper. What I fear is, that he is reserving himself for my next venture—although the story I am now working at is fifty times better than *Gabriel D.*, as, indeed, it can well afford to be.'

Nor was this the only unpleasing notice Oliver's book invoked: one that appeared in the *Saturday Review* (of which there will be something to say hereafter) seems to have wounded his feelings somewhat more than slightly. Writing to Mr. Williams, he says: ' I should be glad to know if *Gabriel Denver* in any way answered the expectations you kindly expressed about it? I have seen many, on the whole, highly favourable reviews—though I am quite aware that these are no absolute gauge of superiority in a commercial point of view: the slashing, if not eccentric, notice which you doubtless saw in the *Saturday* some eight or nine weeks back could not, I should think, have been very favourable to the latter—though more than one mutual friend has tried to argue me into believing it written in a perfectly candid and conciliatory spirit, and as likely to be of use to me, both morally and commercially. I confess honestly that I do not quite see this myself in either light. I shall, in any case, be glad to hear from you with regard to my last book, when you can spare time.'

In reply to this inquiry, Mr. Williams stated that up to that date, July, 1874, only 300 copies of *Gabriel Denver* had been sold, so that the sole advantage received from its publication had been the recognition of its author's powers by the press. Publishers' accounts are mysterious matters which only the elect can understand, so that these figures matter little; it therefore suffices to add that an original copy of *Gabriel Denver* is a rarity difficult to obtain, although there is a cheap reprint procurable. Mr. Williams, to revert to his communication, deprecated any particular attention being paid to the offensive notice, and expressed curiosity to know something about the work Oliver had in hand, making passing allusion to the inestimable advantage possessed by his correspondent in the advice and opinion of such friends as Dante and William Rossetti. This last remark called forth from Oliver, in his next letter, the response: 'I may take this opportunity of explaining that the only advice I ever received as to the course of my stories, either from D. G. Rossetti or his brother William, was the advice, strongly urged by the former, to follow *your* advice with regard to my last book, which he had not then seen. You may remember I was at first disinclined to do this, though I subsequently became more reasonable, and so enabled you to publish the story.' This explanation was undoubtedly dictated by Oliver's intense independence and desire to vindicate his own originality.

*FRIENDSHIP.*

## Oliver Madox Brown.

More than eight years have passed and still, my friend,
  The place thou had'st stands empty in my heart ;
  New friendships come, I know, and they depart,
But ours endures unto the very end.
Oft, battling here, to thee my cry I send,
  If in some distant, conscious world thou art
  I know thy soul will hear that cry and start,
And all the things that are will apprehend,

Because thou wast so close to me so long.
  Nay, hush, my song, thine individual moan !
  Grieve for the whole world whence his light has flown,
His light of splendid sunrise, charged with song.
  Poet and friend and brother, my brother alone—
These words are weak, but, O, my love is strong !
                        PHILIP BOURKE MARSTON.

*February*, 1883.

## CHAPTER V.

### *FRIENDSHIP.*

'We talked about our future many times,
Planned work together, jested, and were grave.'
*A Lament.*—PHILIP BOURKE MARSTON.

ONE of the brightest rays by which Oliver's short springtide of life was lit was his friendship with Mr. Philip Bourke Marston. 'From 1872 till near the end of 1874,' says Mr. Marston,* 'I had the privilege of counting Oliver Madox Brown as my most intimate friend. I had, however, made his acquaintance before the former date, having two years previously met him frequently at his father's house, and at the houses of mutual friends. He was then fifteen, and even at that early age devoted to art. His

\* In *Scribner's Monthly Magazine*, 1876.

manner was remarkable for his boyish straightforwardness; for instance, on hearing any facts which taxed too keenly his credulity, he would deny their authenticity with a blunt frankness characteristic of one even younger. Yet at this time I was struck by his large knowledge of poetry, and the extreme justice of his observations. He selected almost unfailingly, for his special admiration, passages so subtly exquisite that they had often escaped the attention even of professed critics.

'After the period of our first acquaintance,' continues Mr. Marston, 'I did not meet him again until June, 1872, when he asked me to hear a story in manuscript, purporting to be written by a friend of his. The night of his visit I must always now regard with the most tender and melancholy interest. The sweet prolonged summer twilight was almost at an end, and I was sitting quite alone in my study, when Oliver entered. In a short time I perceived that the two years had worked a considerable change in him. The boyish simplicity of his nature was still unchanged; but certain angularities of manner, noticeable before, had been wholly rounded off.

'He often afterwards alluded to that first night of our friendship, recalling the thunderstorm which, imminent in the air, and bursting at length, seemed strangely in harmony with the tale of tempest and passion he had to read.* Not till the reading had been completed, the work discussed and criticized, did he reveal to me its authorship. I was fully prepared for his ultimately achieving great triumphs in the art in which his father has won an undying name; but this manifestation of genius in a direction totally new to him, thoroughly took me by surprise.'

The youthful poet and the young artist-author now became bosom friends, and although they met one another constantly, they maintained a continuous interchange of notes. It can scarcely be claimed for Oliver that he was a letter-writer: he hated correspondence and, as a rule, only followed it up from necessity. He never acquired the natural facility of an accomplished correspondent, although, as an eminent poet (Mr. W. B. Scott) remarks, this might have come later, as he had not yet reached the age when letter-writing is usually entered upon, ere he was snatched away from life. But of his correspondence, whatever its value may be deemed, his friend Philip would appear to have culled the choicest specimens.

Notes of more or less interest seem to have

* The story of *The Black Swan*.

commenced in 1872, and to have been exchanged between the friends until within a week or two of Oliver's death. Until the 24th March, 1873, nothing calling for notice, however, occurs in the correspondence, except occasional allusions to ill-health by the young novelist, in such significant terms as these: 'My head troubles me dreadfully, and renders me utterly incapable of exertion.'

About the above date, Marston wrote to his friend in the following terms, addressing Oliver in the patriarchal way set forth on account of his grave lectures and prudential advice, and subscribing himself 'grandson' for the same reason:—

'MY DEAR GRAN,

I dreamt this morning we were quarrelling furiously. The language employed freely on both sides was, not to put too fine a point on it, more remarkable for power than for elegance.

I was up very early yesterday, and went with my sister to Slough. We walked altogether about eleven miles, and had tea at a delightful old inn, and heard larks, thrushes, and blackbirds all singing together; did they not just sing! I don't think there could have been room to stick another song in, in all the air. We sat under old trees and read Blake. I never knew so fine a day in March before—so full of compassion for what had been and promise for the future. But Nature's promises, on the whole, are just a little more worthless than the promises of men: see in summer what cold wet noons we are led to by exquisite dawns. . . .

I am rather hopeless of making the dogs and the cat friends; Lisette, of the two dogs, being the older and more sagacious, soon knew her (the cat) for what she was and to whom she belonged; but dear Toodles (the little black dog and mine) she exercises a strong fascination on; especially are Toodles' wonder and admiration excited by the splendour of pussy's tail, which she will examine most curiously. Now, a cat like mine does not care about being investigated by what, in her inmost heart, she calls "a little, black, short-coated, sheep-barking toy-terrier." If Lady (that is my cat) could be a little less dignified, Toodles a little less curious, some arrangement might be made.

I remain, with deep respect,<br>
Your dutiful grandson,<br>
FLIP.'

To this communication Oliver responded in his most usual—his humorous strain:—

'My dear Philip,

If you want to make your cat and dogs agree together, catch them, then tie them all up in one large bag, and next hang them to the chandelier over the table of your sitting-room. Should the inmates of the said bag happen to growl at each other, or give any signs whatsoever of mutual discontent, take a big stick, and hit out right and left at them. Hang them up in this fashion for two hours and a half, every day for a fortnight. If, after this, they ever fall out with each other again, *nothing ever will make them friends.**

Yours in great haste,
O. M. B.

* This brilliantly original idea has been suggested by the famous aphorism of the illustrious philosopher, Schopenhauer: " The memory of a common misfortune makes the hardest hearted men love one another." It is to be found in page 1359 of vol. vi. of *The World is Will or Imagination*. Berlin, 1834.'

These facetious remarks were, doubtless, not only called forth by his friend's letter, but as a skit on certain German characteristics, and as the sequence of a discussion between the two young authors. In an epistle of the following month, Oliver indulges in a little more jocularity to this effect:

'I cannot honestly say that I admire the diction of the sentence in your letter to which you especially called my attention. It might be decidedly improved by the addition of a semi-colon, or half a dozen commas. Stick to poetry—it don't want no punctuation: but let prose alone, whatever you do.'

It need scarcely be remarked that these words were intended for pure fun, and that really Oliver was a true admirer of his friend's prose as well as of his poesy, and was, indeed, much interested in all his work. On one occasion Philip was desirous of obtaining a graphic description of an Elizabethan mansion in order to embody it in, or rather to model from it for, a story he was writing. Oliver undertook the labour of love, and wrote the following picturesque delineation of what was wanted:—

'Thurlestone Hall lay in a secluded, densely wooded hollow of the hills, out by the peaceful and antiquated village of Bond (*sic*) Church, in the Isle of Wight. In the year 1849, no other human habitation was visible from the windows of the Hall: the only church lay so far off that you could barely catch sound of its bells on Sunday mornings. For many miles its pleasure-grounds stretched around in lonely, magnificent, and yet well-regulated profusion. Looking out on to the deep blue sea through the great ravine, which fronted the entrance, or back on to the enormous rock-strewn summits of the hills behind, you would have thought Sir Roderick Thurlestone's ancestors, the proud old Earls of Bolton and Lanawar, must have been men of equal affluence and originality, for you could not have chosen a more commanding or bewitching situation along that whole sea-coast, beautiful and desolate though it is. It was a stately red-bricked mansion, faced with grey stone, and built in the reign of our once gracious and Sovereign Lady Queen Elizabeth;—one of those old English country houses which seem made as much for the convenience of the swallows, which take refuge under their eaves, as for the comfort of their own proper inhabitants; full of strange, sinister, wind-bitten crevices and angularities; half-hidden, too, in a luxuriant growth of dark-leaved ivy—so luxuriant, indeed, that its wanton tendrils had crawled up around the very chimneys and run down some of the unused ones. In the spring the apple-orchard in the rear of the house became an almost magical sight; but there were very few of the gnarled old elms among which it stood whose topmost wind-blown branches overlooked its red-tiled roofs.

Usually a perfect and faultless silence reigned all round the place: though you would have heard strange eery sounds about the chambers of the "Hall" on windy nights—shrill, ominous moanings and cries, such as would have made a stranger's very blood run cold in his veins; but the inmates were used to the place, and loved it, may be, for Sir Roderick and his family were seldom absent from the county.'

Written hastily as was this sketch, and left unrevised and in the rough, it has, nevertheless, a flavour of its young author's style about it that is very charming, and produces one of those permanent impressions on the mind objects seen visually frequently imprint, but which written descriptions rarely do: it leaves us desirous of more, and longing to know what quaint, weird legend was attached to the building thus picturesquely portrayed.

On a certain day in April of this same 1873, Oliver is found writing in the following characteristic strain with reference to Marston's projected new volume of poems, *All in All*, a work in which he naturally took great interest:—

'My dear Philip,

.... I should have been round before now to see you myself, only for the last two or three days I have been slightly indisposed. The firm I spoke to you about is ——— and Co. Up to the present day they have only published what they are pleased to term "works on the subject of Fine Art," but in the fulfilment of time they intend to vomit and eject other publications into the astounded world. But at the present they are "not prepared to treat" for the aforesaid publications. Excuse me for not having told you of this ere now: but having been slightly unwell I seem to have forgotten all about the matter. I trust you haven't lost your beautiful cat yet; she is a very creditable beast, but she is not half so grand as mine. The only drawback about mine is that she seems becoming rather selfish: not content with a fair share of the bed, which I have been confined to for the past three days, she does her best to turn me out of it altogether. Now I call this going a trifle too far, as I did my best to explain to the animal. . . .

Oliver Madox Brown.'

The next letter to the same friend, sent on the 19th of May, is interesting from the fact that it contains the germ of what may be termed 'the Nightingale incident' in Oliver's subsequently written romance of *The Dwale Bluth*. Inditing his communication from Lower Merton, he says:

'MY DEAR PHILIP,

I can't turn up at your rooms to-morrow evening. I came down here Saturday morning, and am going on to Dorking this afternoon. Shall not be back till Thursday. I'll bring you back two or three " Dorking fowls," if I can catch any.

Speaking of fowls reminds me that I haven't slept a wink here all night. There is a large chestnut-tree outside my bedroom window—the blossoms of which have erected themselves finely by now—and hidden by the dense foliage of this tree, a godless and dissipated nightingale persisted in filling the air of the night with " harmony," until I wished it at the very devil. I tried to fling my jug of water over it; but this made slight difference, for the rain was coming down in a perfect deluge at the time; so the disreputable and conceited beast only screamed the louder. I suppose it took me to be some blockhead of a Philistine critic, for it defied me in a truly Swinburnian fashion, and was, no doubt, wonderfully satirical. Just before sunrise it desisted; and, as I thought, took flight for good. But, alas! it came back soon after with two others: and then the trio seemingly began a violent fight!—during the progress of which they sang louder than ever.

It's astonishing how cantankerous these birds seem to be! I know you like them: in fact, I remember your having once informed me of the existence of a kind of "elective affinity" between yourself and the nightingale tribe, so I give you these little details in order that you may learn what they really are. I've no sympathy for song-birds myself—more especially when they keep one awake—it's even worse than being sent to sleep by them.

O. M. B.'

It was not Marston, as Oliver was of course aware, but another poet of our era, who claimed 'elective affinity' with the nightingale, but the point was too good to be passed over. His next letter refers chiefly to Philip Marston's projected new volume of poems, and apart from its interest in that direction is attractive as showing the anxiety—also displayed in other ways—Oliver experienced on behalf of his friend's success.

'My dear Philip,

Just a line in great haste to tell you I've seen . . . . to-day, and (have) been speaking with him about the volume of yours which he has. I am very, *very* glad to say that he really seems to appreciate the poetry in it, and thinks it very beautiful. The only thing he is uncertain about is that he thinks it will make rather a small volume. He has not quite finished with it, and I thought you wouldn't mind my leaving it with him for a day or two longer. . . . I've no doubt he'll be able to serve you in some way. I know he had a very high opinion of your other volume; but he told me that he thought this a very great advance upon it. I've just been looking over Graves's book; some of its contents are very charming. My proofs are coming in now faster and faster—like damned souls in hell. I get more and more disgusted every moment. . . .'

Another communication, sent, apparently, about the 10th of September, after referring to the same subject of his friend's new work, launches out into one of those humorous, highly exaggerated narratives, Oliver so delighted to relate. The epistle runs thus:

'MY DEAR PHILIP,
    I have just seen . . . . who has brought your MS. back from Kelmscott. Rossetti has not gone quite through the book; but he and . . . .

spent several evenings over it with great pleasure and satisfaction. The sonnets were chiefly liked and read. Rossetti in fact seems to have been very much impressed by them.

. . . . . is this week going to call on C—— about the book . . . . he seems quite to have set his mind on bringing the book through in some form or other, and I have very little doubt of his succeeding.

What a frightful thing it is to keep house all by one's self! The silence and monotony of living all alone in a big house is so depressing that I sometimes think of going and jumping down the back staircase by way of varying it a little. The absence of sound is so intense that the ticking of the hall-clock is audible from the top of the roof. Last night, however, the servants made enough row to satisfy the D—— himself. It appears that they secretly gave a dinner-party, and arranged to give a little ball after it. As far as I could make out, the ladies and gentlemen who had not been asked to the dinner considered themselves grievously insulted, and commenced making themselves very disagreeable to those who had been. Two gentlemen, respectable and married, challenged each other on the spot; and adjourning to the pavement, did their little best to knock each other's brains out on it. I came home unexpectedly about one o'clock and found them in this position, with the rest of the company looking on through the area railings. The wives of the above-mentioned combatants were only held from tearing each other's eyes out by main force. Just imagine such a scene in a respectable household!

Of course I remonstrated with the cook in the morning. The creature burst into tears, and said that if this was the way I treated her "after hall the nice little puddin's and custards she'd been making me for the past week, she didn't know what I'd come to."

What could I say after this? I can't bear to see a woman in tears! Don't you pity your unfortunate friend,

OLIVER M. BROWN?'

And, strange to say, Master Oliver does not appear to have ever betrayed the weeping cook or her accomplices, nor does the whole truth of this skirmish at the area railings in Fitzroy Square—which happened during the temporary absence on account of ill health of the faithful Charlotte—seem ever to have reached the ears of any members of the 'respectable household' after their return to town. In his reply to this letter, Marston says: 'All that you tell me about

'. . . . and Rossetti is very gratifying. I am proud to know they like my book. It is consoling to hear that . . . . will try and carry the matter through. . . . I think the party at your house must have been great fun. I can sympathize thoroughly with your feeling of loneliness, for my room seems terribly dreary when my sister goes away, and I find, as you do, the silence quite unbearable. I was in bed last night by twelve o'clock; but don't be frightened—it was the beginning of no reform. What a fearful thing it would be if we did reform and became proper members of society; but I don't think we need be alarmed. What nice letters you write. Will you come and see me on Monday? . . . Don't have a headache, or gout, or any ailment, mental or physical. I want to hear from you the words of wisdom, and to be instructed by you in the way in which I should go.'

The above extract gives a slight hint of what in a letter written by Oliver to Philip towards the end of October in this year may clearly be detected, one very palpable cause of the lad's headaches, and the reason of his frequent complaints to his correspondent of ill-health. After explaining his inability to keep an appointment made for the following Sunday, Oliver says: 'I trust sincerely that I am not putting you out in any particularly troublesome way—but, "alas! I have no control over my destiny!" as the heroes of romance usually say when they have committed any particularly abominable crime.' And he proceeds, 'When I see you again we really must arrange some plan by which you will agree to let me go away at twelve o'clock in future, when I come to your rooms. I am as ill as possible to-day, owing to sitting up till four last night; and never will I do the like again, though I live to be a hundred and three. Your martyrized friend.'

'My dear Noll,' was the chaffing rejoinder, 'what is this wonderful and mysterious engagement that so jostles aside an engagement of nearly ten days' standing? . . . You amuse me excessively by your earnest pleading to be let away early! If you remember, when you came to see me on Tuesday, you remarked early in the evening that you "should like to go not later than one," and though it may seem to you now incredible, and altogether impossible to believe, I replied, without even fainting or even changing colour, that you should go just when you wished, and as I answered you then I shall always answer you. . . . If your extreme ill-health, and numerous and mysterious engagements will let you come to me on Monday, I shall be very pleased to see you. Always yours very sincerely, P. B. M.' To this Oliver immediately replied: 'Pray forgive me, but I find the reasons which I imagined were going to keep me at home Sunday morning are no longer in existence, so please be ready at a quarter to twelve, as before decided. I have, as is usually the case with me, behaved very selfishly and impolitely, yet I hope you will overlook this in consideration of my sincere repentance. Doubtless, I shall end on the treadmill, or in a madhouse, as my father is in the habit of telling me at times. I will tell you why I fancied I should have to stop at home on Sunday morning when I see you. You will be quite satisfied of my plain dealing and unquestionable veracity.'

Writing to his friend on the 8th of November, the young novelist says:

'My dear Philip,

I have been out every blessed evening this week, and I really don't feel up to coming out to-night again. Will you allow me, therefore, to come Tuesday night instead? Just write and tell me if I may. You will be glad to hear my book is out at last. . . . I am very proud of the following quotation for the heading of the chapter I am now writing on. What do you think of it?——"A worthy axium hath been surmized—*O Reader!*—and a will deserving of Inquisition. That (In this Worlde):—Either thou mayest act accordant to thine owne welfare, thus bringing to pass the detryment of Others: Or to thine owne proper detryment, that these Others may come about to Profit thereby: And (forsooth!) that there existeth none other Rule of Life."—"*The Devyle's Owne Touchstone: Being an infallible Sevenfolde Exposition thereof.* Englished by J. Sparrow, barrister of the Inner Temple, from the German, 1647."

This will, doubtless, remind you of my costermonger's story: but it is from Jacob Böhme himself. It proves, however, what an upright and just-spirited man that said costermonger was—leaving out the oaths, of course. . . .

     OLIVER MADOX BROWN.'

The following note appears to have been Philip's reply to the deferred appointment,—

'MY DEAR NOLL,

   I may go to Reading to-morrow with my father, but I shall be back in my rooms at eleven, if you like to chance it. We shall not go if it is cold or a fog. I have been made very happy by the kindest letter from Rossetti, respecting a little poem which, I think I told you, was written by a friend of mine, and published in *Good Words*. What a supreme man is Rossetti! Why is he not some great exiled king, that we might give our lives in trying to restore him to his kingdom! I wonder shall I ever be able to let him know how I love and honour him! You seemed to me dull at the concert, old boy; I hope nothing was wrong. You know what pleasure your visits give me, and now, very sincerely,

I am yours,<br>P. B. M.'

On the 19th Oliver wrote to ask Marston if he had seen the review—the first out—of *Gabriel Denver*, in the *Academy*, 'from the justice-dealing hand of that amaranthine and comfortable luminary, Mr. Simcox?' A few days later, when less satisfactory critiques had appeared, he wrote:—

'MY DEAR PHILIP,

I have been slightly unwell for the past five or six days; so that (particularly as I have only got up to-day for the first time since Friday evening) you will understand my reluctance to venture out into the infernal fog at present rampaging round Fitzroy Square and its vicinity. After God . . . . having given . . . . the sun, moon, earth, etc., in such agreeable juxtaposition, it seems hard that a fog like this should be capable of interposing its impertinent self and cutting them off so completely from one another! . . . . Excuse the obviously shaky condition of this epistle.—O. M. B. . . . .'

'I called on Mr. Swinburne the other day, and found that he had gone to Henley-on-Thames, having been very ill for several days previously, according to the housekeeper. . . . I am sorry to say that there has been an article on him in some Transatlantic "Libel Gazette," of a very base, scurrilous, description; written and signed by an eccentric friend of Mr. C. K. Miller, (one "Olive Harper" by name; a blonde-haired, strong-minded, and slightly mendacious female party, who has been "making tracks," to use her own expression, through various European capitals; and writing astounding reports thereof to her native journals,) which contains—among certain matters obviously evolved from her own self-consciousness—certain other matters which . . . . declares can only have come from the evil speaking lips of Mr. Miller *lui-même*.

If this be true Mr. Miller must be a cad of the very lowest description. I have a very poor opinion of him through certain other matters, but I hardly like to believe this—for that he possesses great talent only Mr. J. himself would deny.'

About the middle of December, writing to excuse a with him not very unusual fit of forgetfulness, Oliver explains, 'I was writing all night, and forgot all about your letter till I left off at half-past two, when, of course, it was *too* late, let alone the fact that it was raining hard.'

On the 27th of the same month, after making some seasonable gratulations, Oliver indulges in a little literary tittle-tattle, anent an amusing attempt made by some friends of his to concoct a sonnet in imitation of certain peculiarities of style supposed to appertain to the author of *Paracelsus*. 'A great friend of Mr. Robert Browning,' is his mock earnest assertion, 'was telling us a great deal concerning Mr. Browning's new poem, which seems about to appear—the opening of which consists of a series of Shakespearian sonnets. Of the first, entitled *Past Chronology*, he possesses the MS., and he was kind enough to permit me to copy it. Now, I am not a bad hand at these here kind of things, but I'll be hanged if I can make head or tail of it! Can you? I fancy it must refer to something in the construction or plot of the story which follows, so that it would most likely be unfair to judge or read it without the context. Isn't it stupendous?' A copy of the pseudo-Browning sonnet accompanied the communication, and is now reproduced for the edification of our readers:

> A chronologic skull, sir! 'twas a poet's;
>    But 'tother's wasn't my friend's friend's, I say.
> Our first a Lombard were the wind to blow its
> Loudest, could not daunt him, loved to pray
> Too, in all the English language is no rhyme
> Describes him thoroughly. You should have watched him knit
> Those brows of his, black brows, sir, scarred by time
> And scowling like a pent-house. But your sonnet
> Should have a moral, let's to it, tooth and nail.
> You'd never catch it, were you to fall on it
> Without premeditation. Work like a snail
> Gnawing a lotus leaf, you're on the brink of it—
> How now, Sir Numbskull, turn and think of it.

The first letter of the series appertaining to 1874 is dated January the 15th, and although lit up with Oliver's wonted 'pawky' humour, contains, as usual, allusions to his ill-health. 'I don't think I shall be able to get out for two or three nights yet,' it begins, 'as I am afflicted with a hoarse sore throat, which prevents me speaking. Couldn't you manage to turn up here some evening? We shall all be delighted to see you. I have just been forced to swallow a wine-glassful of the most disgusting medicine

I ever tasted—which is saying something. It smells like a combination of old gas-pipe, nicotine, and turpentine, with a dash of peppermint and garlic to flavour it. My unfortunate cat demanded, as usual, a share of what I was partaking of—but, oh! the expression of her face when I gave her the glass to smell!'

In a letter to Oliver, sent in the month of February, Philip Marston alluded to a disturbance which had occurred next door. A policeman had been summoned but declined to enter the house unless one of the disturbers cried 'murder.' Eventually one of them, a female, did scream the necessary word, when the place was entered and quietude restored. In the course of his letter, Mr. Marston also asked whether there is 'anything in the poetry of L. E. L., and why she is so written up?' One of the usual exaggerated, humorous epistles was elicited, containing the following remarks: 'I am sorry to hear of your neighbour's obstreperousness—my conscience stings me somewhat in the matter; for if he *did* succeed in doing for the young lady you mention, I, who by tapping on the wall with my walking-stick apparently aggravated him to madness, must in a moral sense be responsible for the deed. Never mind; God's will be done! Who L. E. L. was is a profound, inexplicable mystery, as far as I am concerned; she was an authoress of some talent, my father says, and was, I believe, unfortunate in some fashion or other—went mad, or was eaten by the natives of the Sandwich Islands, or something or other. It isn't difficult to invent an end for her; but I really don't know anything whatever of the matter.' In this letter was returned a Stores-ticket, belonging to the late Arthur O'Shaughnessy, Mr. Philip B. Marston's brother-in-law, which Oliver had borrowed, and which he now sent back with some of his customary banter, such as, 'I swore solemnly to my identity with your sister's husband. They seemed to think I'd got rather untidy since I was there last, or had changed in some way.'

The next communication carries the correspondence up to the end of April, and shows Oliver still as interested and as anxious as ever —despite his 'poking fun at him'—about his friend's literary projects. 'Dear Philip,' he rattles on, 'I find I shan't be able to come tomorrow (or rather the day after to-morrow) evening, no how. I am so sorry; but I propose and my mother disposes, just at present. I hope you will think over the affair of—— and—— (publishers), while there yet remains time; you will have a splendid chance of playing one off against the other if you are dissatisfied . . . the *strictest secrecy* must be preserved, of course. I think your father's notions are too *strait-laced*—he seems rather like my own father, in fact. There is no good in dealing honestly with publishers—you must oppose fraud to fraud, swindling to swindling, villainy to villainy, if you mean to get anything out of them. I should even recommend violence, if need be.—Ever yours, O. M. B.'

Another note from Oliver, referring to the same business, and written about the same time, begins in a more serious strain, although it rapidly reverts to the customary humorous tone: it is undated and reads thus :—

'DEAR PHILIP,

I am most anxious to learn if any communications have again passed between yourself and C——? . . . Write me a line if you have any news.

My father came back unexpectedly while I was out last night, and had to tackle the door as Jupiter did the Titans—with thunderbolts, or the nearest approach he could make to them for half an hour. I was out and the rest in bed. . . .

Ever yours most faithfully,
O. M. B.'

## A SLIGHT MISUNDERSTANDING.

Friends are as sensitive as lovers, and are therefore as likely to have 'tiffs.' Words, which if spoken by a stranger or by a mere acquaintance, would float unnoted by, when uttered by a dear one, wound deeply, and if not quickly medicined, rankle sorely. Some slight 'difference,' happily cured by the speedy and drastic measures of both concerned, is foreshadowed by the following correspondence which passed between Oliver and Philip during the latter part of July. Philip's letter is as follows :—

*Sunday Night.*

MY DEAR OLIVER,

That no misunderstanding may arise between us, and that our friendship may be done full justice to, I write to say that you hurt me deeply on Thursday night, for I must tell you what I thought perhaps you would have known, that those poems are, to me at least, sacred; they can bear no jesting allusion, far less allusions which go still further. I have written this not without pain to myself, and I have, you see, been quite frank with you. I leave town on Thursday, I think, and I shall be very pleased to see you between now and then, if you can manage it.

Yours sincerely,

PHILIP BOURKE MARSTON.'

In response to this remonstrance for the unintentional infliction of pain, the warm-hearted youth instantly returned the following manly letter :—

'My dear Philip,

It gives me the greatest sorrow to think I should ever (unwittingly) have made any single allusion to your poems which could in any way be capable of wounding your feelings. I have always prized your poetry at its highest worth, and I am exceedingly glad you give me an opportunity of confirming the many words I have spoken on the subject, both to yourself and others—as of apologizing for a misunderstood inadvertence in my speech, of which I should otherwise have not been cognizant. I will come round Tuesday evening. Till then, with all best wishes,

Yours as ever,
Oliver Madox Brown.'

The offence, so frankly proclaimed and so promptly repaired, was instantly obliterated from the minds of the two friends, who became, if it were possible, more friendly than ever.

*LIFE IN LONDON AND LECHLADE.*

# Defuit.

In Spring I rambled through an Alpine land,
   And in snow-hollows marked a print of feet,
   A youth's elastic footsteps : screened from heat
Of sunshine, death-white snow on either hand.
Impenetrable heaven unmeasured spanned
   The crags where mountain-sheep and lambkins bleat.
   Turning a point where bay with yew leaves meet,
To hear an eagle scream I took my stand.
There to the sheer edge of a precipice
   That foot-track reached and ceased. A cairn of stones
   Was piled and lettered 'No man found his bones.'
   A village-girl at twilight sang a song
   In youthful and in manful passion strong—
And said, ' The youth who vanished taught me this."

W. M. ROSSETTI.

*April* 1883.

## CHAPTER VI.

### *LIFE IN LONDON AND LECHLADE.*

' London I never loved for London's sake,
　Her crowds oppressed me more than solitude ;
But some far music his fine ear could take,
　Mine failed to catch ; yea, since he found her good,
Loved the strong ebb and flow of fluctuant life,
The night's uneasy calm, the day's loud strife,
Found all her ancient streets with memories rife,
　Shall I not love her too, asleep, awake ?'
　　　　*A Lament.*—PHILIP BOURKE MARSTON.

A SOMEWHAT retrospective glance must be taken across that interval of Oliver's life which his correspondence with Philip Marston covers. In September, 1872, when negotiations for offering *Gabriel Denver* to Messrs. Smith, Elder and Co. were opened with Mr. Smith Williams, the youthful author informed that gentleman that for more than three months he had been engaged on a second romance, a story of Devonshire country life. This story, afterwards to be known as *The Dwale Bluth*, subsequent events caused Oliver to put on one side for some months, and apparently without reluctance, for, as he wrote to Mr. Williams, 'doubtless at the end of that time I could see my way to making a great many alterations, which I should scarcely care to effect without some little time for consideration.'

The two months or so spent in hacking and hewing from his initial romance its pristine glory, caused Oliver to lose interest for a while in his Devonshire novel, and to divert his energies to the composition of ' an entirely new story of a somewhat more dramatic order—the end of which will,' he wrote Mr. Smith Williams, 'in some degree resemble the conclusion of *Gabriel Denver*. I am not quite certain about a title for it as yet,' he added, 'but I think of calling it *To All Eternity*. If you think this would sound too vague or bombastic, the book might simply be named after its heroine, *Agnes Desborough*. There will be no retrospective writing in the course of this story, if it can possibly be avoided, and, as the scene is laid in London, there will be no opportunity for indulging in too many descriptive passages, although there are many aspects of London street-scenery which have been hitherto utterly overlooked and neglected. I hope you will allow me to send you the first two or three chapters as soon as I can work them into shape.'

The new story of London life thus shadowed forth ultimately took shape under the title of *Hebditch's Legacy,* but the germ of it also budded forth into a poem—haplessly for us, but a fragment. *To All Eternity,* in its poetic form, was to enunciate the belief that—

> 'There's no standard
> In heaven above or hell beneath, o'er which
> A woman's soul may not predominate—
> May not aspire to—or degrade itself!'

But little of this theory in verse has been preserved, even if much were written; but from the virile and vigorous lines which are extant is learnt that the heroine's eyes

> 'Kindled and shone like flames blown in the wind.
> . . . . . . . They made
> A boy's soul luminous, where now they burn
> The grown man's soul to death!'

This fine imagery is followed by a magnificent burst of passion, which, though called forth by the oldest theme of human song, sounds as if drawn from the crushed lees of a full-lived man's experience, rather than from the intuitive feelings of a mere lad:

> 'Ah love! love! love!
> Whose unintelligible promptings lure

Earth's mightiest nerves to thraldom—whose deep magic,
Too swift for timorous afterthought, too deep
For present doubt, makes blind the brain—whose hands
Mould this man's heaven from that man's hell—whose gaze
Infatuates—whose wind-shod feet resume
The joys its hands disperse—whose yearnings storm
Heaven with their high intentions, ere God paves
Hell's wildest depths with them!'

This passionate outbreak is followed by a charming picture of forest scenery and quiet woodland life, as opposite in tone and tenor as can well be devised. The story and the heroine are both thus naturally, yet artistically, introduced:

'The wood
Grew thinner thereabouts—for presently
I broke into a glade where the warm sun
Pierced through at random, and, just slipping round
The weather-beaten trunk of a huge oak,
Stepped out into the light. How shall I tell
What happened there? For first I stood half-dazed
In one great blaze of sunlight. Then there came
A sharp stroke on my side, and I reeled back,
Breathless and stupefied; whilst a shrill scream
Rang in mine ears. Just hovering past my face
I saw the suspended figure of a girl
Nigh grown to womanhood mount high i' the air
Some moments yet ere she could stay herself.
She had been swinging as she sang, her rope
Fast to the boughs o'erhead; and I, it seemed,
Had stepped before her unawares, her song
Still on her lips low-lingering; till it changed
Into that frightened scream. And now she stopped,
Sprang to the earth, and disappeared ere I
Could gain my feet again; I only caught
One brief glance of her face—then she was gone.'

And with this short episode the fragment finishes, it being only just long enough to prove that the author, had he lived and laboured at poesy, might therein have fully rivalled his success in prose.

The story styled *Hebditch's Legacy* does not appear to us equally attractive with Oliver's other longer works, and, indeed, in its present condition, fails to take such hold on the imagination as does the weirdly fascinating *Black Swan*, or that sweetly human, albeit unfinished masterpiece, *The Dwale Bluth*. *Hebditch's Legacy*, which was never completed by its author, and had, therefore, to be made up by his editors from notes or remembrance of what he had said, runs too much in the common groove of ordinary fiction to exercise that wonderful charm originality only can wield. Its complicated plot needs more space for working out than the limits within which its author left it, whilst the story itself deals too much with hidden wills, conventional coincidences, and the usual paraphernalia of three volume sensation-mongers. Its chief drawback, apart from the fact of its unfinishedness, is that it competes too closely with the productions of the ordinary routine novelist; yet, as the composition of a boy in his teens, it is, like nearly all Oliver's work, simply marvellous.

Indeed, *Hebditch's Legacy* contains many fine bits of portraiture, characteristic glimpses of deep thought, and some clever descriptive word-painting. Several of the personages in this novel, we are assured, were drawn from life, and the sketch of the lawyer, Mr. Blackoder, was accurately copied from a veritable solicitor, as will readily be believed by those who read it. He is introduced as sitting in his office, where 'the light of his lamp fell full on his face, in which that strange look, theoretically so essential to success in life, the look of the man who knows the value of silence, was unmistakably visible. For success, in its ordinary sense, consists not so much in talking yourself as in making others talk. This man's swarthy skin, emphasizing the greyness of his hair, plainly indicated the traces of some foreign (perhaps even Eastern) blood in his veins; his eyes, grey, piercingly luminous, and never still for an instant, possessed that penetrating, yet indirect, look which we inseparably connect with the Oriental physiognomy. Not the faintest shadow of an emotion seemed discernible in them. His black crooked shadow, cast high up on the wall behind, craned over him furtively; so still and motionless that it grew at last like some evil familiar spirit, trying to guess what new wizardry its master could have found to ponder over.'

The death-bed scene in Mrs. Helmore's chamber is most powerfully told, and affects us as if described direct from nature; and who can believe such remarks as follow to proceed from aught but actual observation?

'Nothing in all nature seems more weird or fantastic than the delirium, born of prolonged exhaustion, which so often precedes the death brought about by consumption. Perhaps one should hardly term it delirium at all; as the mind breaks down with the failure of the body, its imagination seems to strengthen and gain force, until at last the sense of life merges into a dream, and the profound last sleep falls upon it. A form of death long drawn out and with an incredibly unexpected ending! The whole room was filled with her quick, difficult breathing—it was like the rasping of a file. To judge from her face, she must have been young still—scarcely thirty-three, perhaps. Once she might have been beautiful, but now her features were emaciated in the extreme, the eyes sunken, and the cheeks utterly hollowed and wasted away. For others, the light and frivolity of life; for her, the solemnity and pathos of death; for others, the radiance; for her, the *silence* of the sun. At times one can discover beauty in a dying face such as might baffle description. The complexion grows so diaphanous, the eyes glitter so strangely, that quite at last the first vague rays of some new existence seem fallen on the features:

> '" Some say that gleams of a remoter world
> Visit the soul in sleep,—that death is slumber;
> And that its dreams the busy thoughts outnumber
> Of those that wake and live."

Or it often happens that the act of death looks as though the body were dissolving away and leaving the soul behind—rather than the soul the body.

'But here it was otherwise: a profound, unendurable horror of death, as it were, lay on all the features—death, which had stamped them for its own so unmistakably; her lips quivering and muttering incessantly, her eyes dilated and filled with sombre, unluminous fire, as though her whole life had been as a flame—self-consuming —and those eyes were the last particles left of it.'

That that London, whose street scenery presented, according to his own words, many aspects utterly overlooked and neglected, had received his deep study, numberless touches in this novel of *Hebditch's Legacy* evince; take, for instance, the fine description of the metropolis in a fog:—

Early one November afternoon . . . an immense squalid volume of fog swept down across the central parishes of London; blocking out the residue of the brief wintry sunlight, and suffocating their crowded, tumultuous thoroughfares. It was as though some horrid dream, some dismal nightmare, had suddenly enthralled the town; it was *tohu va bohu* realized again, for London is essentially the city of dyspepsia—of morbid self-torturing imagination; and there are certain days towards the fall of the year on which its sense of degradation and of misery appears to transcend all bounds—grown too uncontrollably poignant even for suppression. Sinister and poisonous, and hiding the sun away, it seemed just such a vapour as that which once upon a time rolled forth and embodied itself from the magic jar of Suleyman—unsealed by the Arab fisherman—a sullen, long imprisoned monster, an Efreet, consecrating its recovered liberty only in the blood of its deliverer. Or it was as though the houses had been swept off the visible face of the earth by some stupendous conflagration—emptied and dissolved into the drifts of lurid smoke that yet enwrapped their ruins. All the atmosphere was full of vague palpitating sounds and rumours. In the streets (save for the city link-bearers, round whose torches the flame-irradiated vapour—*florentia lumina flammis*—seemed to take fire and glare so fantastically) men lost sight of each other's corporeal identities, or shrank into mere sound-creating shadows. Every visible object became the disembodied phantom of some former self. The fog was at its worst round Chancery Lane. . . . Ere long the whole centre of London seethed into one illimitable chaos.

'Clifford's Inn, never an animated spot at the brightest seasons, under the paralyzing unwholesome tutelage of this fog, grew dreary and dilapidated indeed. The soot-corroded corners of its houses looked gloomily through the nauseous obscurity; the skeleton-silhouettes of what were once its trees (dotted still with the last nests of a once populous rookery, clothed with fog in lieu of foliage, and shrivelled in their winter's atrophy) looked more like weeds, stagnating in the mud-discoloured depths of some Brobdingnagian horsepond. What the rooks, which then patronized the "Inn," did with themselves that day, Heaven alone knows! At last, towards four—saving one dimly lighted window, whose vague rays produced an aureole round its sills such as might once have graced the brows of a rebellious angel—its whole interior courtyards were blurred together and blotted out of sight.'

Another phase of London life noted by the youth's observant eye is thus pointed out: 'A large crowd had collected round them already, strange to say. No better idea of the immensity of London can be acquired than by watching the way in which one of these crowds swarms together in a street where previously no single soul seemed visible. In this fog it looked more mysterious than ever. A crowd rises in London like a cloud in the sky—it comes one knows not whence, and seems to dissolve back again into bricks and mortar.'

But finer far than these metropolitan *chiaroscuro* sketches are the brilliant little snatches of thought with which the *Legacy* is begemmed, as, 'once more in the sunlight . . . his shadow (which hitherto had stopped modestly outside at the entrance) flew to his feet again;' and such original similes as 'the moonbeams shrank back through the intersecting boughs like the horns of a disturbed snail, leaving all the garden in perfect darkness.' And still finer thoughts and veritably grand conceptions are imbedded in this, as in all Oliver's work. Take, for instance, the following picturesque description, which none but an artist with a poet's eye—or poet with an artist's hand—could have written:

'There still exists a sketch in pencil—in the

possession of some friend or relative—by an artist who died comparatively young*—a sketch entitled *Man and His Conscience*, which represents two wild-visaged figures, stark stripped and running swiftly down the damp sand of a desolate sea-beach; one in the footsteps of the other. It might have been designed by Michelangelo. The waves are an inspiration in themselves; wild, cold, and inveterate, a few strokes of the pencil have set them dashing and surging for ever. Behind, the sky—grey, dumb, speechbound, as it were—"aweary with her wings"—leans vaporously on the horizon, and rests there. The whole sketch is filled with the monotony and foam-speckled desolation of these waves, and with the steel-grey frozen neutrality of the horizon beyond; with the sense of movement and of gradually quickening flight. You can hear the waves hiss through the pebbles—the wind whistles round the limbs and the nakedness of the fugitives. And nothing else save these two figures visible — subtly designed; incredibly swift in action; one running in the other's footsteps. Where will the race end ? Will the pursuer ever look fully in the eyes of the pursued, as he strains to do even now ? Will the foremost be forced to remove the convulsive fingers from

* David Scott, R.S.A.

his ears? Will the one who follows unburthen his tight-shut lips at last? None can tell! It may perhaps be they will face each other in some final goal (out of sight now and to all eternity)—when the fatal sea, rising, will drive them in, till they can run no further—where they may be friends at last: while the waves will sweep them away in their embraces and their reconciliation, even as it now consumes the mutual footprints of their hostility and flight.

'This sketch is an epitome of the human mind —what soul so guiltless who has not undergone these struggles once. . . .

'How is it possible that things so visible to one mind are not real and visible to all others? How can it be that the secret which burns for ever on the lips has never yet found utterance— unconsciously in sleep—in momentary forgetfulness? No. The soul flies, the accuser pursues: and the soul (the body's identity) day after day follows its occupations, and mingles in the turmoil of the city and the haunts of its fellow-men—each with his own heart gnawing perhaps . . .

'But it is a result of civilization, that no man having once done wrong can escape the moral consequences of his action—unless, indeed, he be not mentally responsible for it: unless his mind be deranged—for the nerves vibrate perpetually to it, and the brain never forgets its wrong-doing. The punishment is so severe for infringement of the laws in force, the fall so terrible, the mingling of the mental and physical agony so intense—and the discovery, above all, so easy, so overwhelmingly imminent—that there can be no rest after, save in the severest toil and bodily ailment.'

How the youth acquired the psychological insight to fit him to say these things is a wonder, for no amount of training—nothing but experience, one would deem—could have driven these results of matured reasoning into his brain. Although in this 'Hamlet of the Centuries' such speculations are rife, and in Edgar Poe's *Man of the Crowd* some such mental contemplation of conscience is indulged in, the originality of Oliver Madox Brown's views cannot be gainsaid.

But it is necessary to dismiss *Hebditch's Legacy*, and, for a while, turning from the literary aspects of Oliver's career, revert to more directly personal matters. In such a life as was his, so happy but so short, there seems little left to chronicle beyond the production of his romances and the analysis of his personal story as divulged in his correspondence, so naïve and simple as it is as contrasted with the experience and virility of his mental life. In the early summer of 1873 he is found writing to his sister Lucy, then travelling in Italy, in the following terms:

'My dear Lucy,

I don't know how to excuse myself for not having written to you long ere this, but we have been so occupied with one thing and another that I have scarcely known whether I was standing on my head or on my heels. Papa and mamma are now away at Kelmscott, and the house is dreadfully dull and lonely. I am just correcting the last of my proofs, though I am sorry to say that what with one thing and another the book has been so delayed that its owners "think best to reserve it for the autumn," as Mr. Williams has just informed me. However, there is plenty of time, I suppose.

I am very pleased to learn how you are enjoying yourself; but you mustn't exaggerate your adventures *too* much when you return. I am fully resolved to make a trip somewhere abroad myself if the next " romance " sells well. Mr. W. was talking about it as though he were quite prepared to treat for it when finished.

I really can't think of anything to tell you, excepting that J. C. Hotten, the publisher, is dead, which . . . . may like to hear.

Thank you for the nightshade. I have just been hearing a story read by the elder brother of the Mackays, which seems full of promise and talent. It is just a sketch, but a very clever one. I should fancy from the look of him that he lacks the perseverance and invention necessary to get through anything more mature or longer.

Papa has just finished a wonderful chalk drawing of old Mr. Miller. Are you doing any professional work? I suppose you have very little time to think of that. Have you recognised much of Rome? One often retains a perfect memory of things seen in childhood, without remembering where one has seen them, until coming upon them again one finds that they coincide exactly with the remembrance of them. It is quite startling sometimes to find that a place one has supposed only to exist in one's own imagination has really a material existence of its own. What wonderful enigmas childrens' minds are! I don't think they have ever been analyzed or understood properly. You must excuse the bad handwriting of this letter —as, also, the jerky and involved style of it— for I have got a severe headache; although I put off writing to you for so long that I am ashamed to delay it any longer. Trusting that this will reach you safely, and with kindest regards to all your party, believe me, my dear Lucy,

   Your very affectionate brother,
     OLIVER MADOX BROWN.'

In a letter written to his father about the same time as that just quoted, he again adverts to the suggestion that his next novel is to pass into the hands of the publishers of his first, remarking that their reader had spoken about the story Oliver was then engaged on 'as though it were quite settled that it was to be published by his own firm: for he begged me,' he says, 'not to send it them too quickly, "as it never did to publish two works by the same author without some little time intervening between the dates of publication." They would be prepared for it by about January or December.'

During the progress of his romance Oliver found it necessary to refer to various works of an out-of-the-way nature, works which he did not possess, and might find it difficult, or even impossible, to procure. Naturally, he thought of visiting the British Museum Reading-room, that resort of all in similar difficulty—that epitome of human wit, wisdom, and folly. He appears to have applied for a ticket of admission in the usual way, but was met by an unforeseen obstacle; he was labouring under the delightful drawback of youth; he was still in his teens, and no person could be admitted as a reader until he had attained his majority—had reached the magical age of one-and-twenty! Oliver Madox Brown, having some knowledge of his own powers, feeling the real need of his requirements, and well aware of the trivial nature of many persons' studies at the Reading-room, deemed that the exercise of a little personal influence—that great lever of English life—would obtain him what he wanted—entrance to the bibliographists' paradise. But he was as quickly undeceived as was Moore's Peri: the laws of the Museum, if not as stringent as those of Media and Persia, were not to be departed from for the sake of genius, however brilliant.

Appealing to a literary friend for advice, he received a characteristic reply, in which were these remarks: 'With regard to the officials of the British Museum, I don't know that I can blame them very severely. The Museum, like Nature herself, is governed by general, not special laws, and if among the thousand nineteen-year-olds who would if they could turn the Reading-room into a bear-garden, there now and then turns up one who is a genius—why, genius is always an anomaly of which general laws take no cognizance, and can take none. Neither Nature nor man's institutions can take the casuistic view of affairs. I forget what is the age under which admittance is refused, but if it is twenty, I fear that appeal would not stand much chance. Perhaps I may be able to get some of the books you want.'

Unfortunately, man's institutions do not recognise the anomaly of genius, and very resolutely turn their backs upon such a disturbing element when Nature so far forgets herself as to introduce it; therefore Oliver's remonstrance, or appeal, or whatever it may be termed, was not successful, and owing to the mishap of youth—the one mishap which all legislators would envy him—he could not become a visitor at the British Museum Reading-room.

Amongst the works needed for his guidance were some of a legal character, and as he could not be admitted to the Museum Library, Mr. J. Winter Jones, then principal Librarian—at the suggestion of Oliver's friend, Mr. Richard Garnett—kindly forwarded him a letter of introduction to the Superintendent of the Inner Temple Library. This recommendatory letter, however, Oliver does not appear to have made use of, by this time, probably, having been sickened of the whole affair, and obliged to execute his work in the best way he could, without resort to any of these carefully environed institutions.

His ineffectual attempt to break down the barriers of routine terminated at the end of October, 1873, and for some months there are no further *data* of Oliver's life beyond those already given in the correspondence with his friend Philip. On a certain Monday, early in 1874, he indited one of his wonted humoristic epistles to a lady friend, using such boyish *badinage* as this:—

'I was quite taken by surprise, while surreptitiously reading your last letter to Lucy this afternoon, at coming across an unexpected allusion to your son and heir's nose, eyes, and other personal appendages—for it appears that I had quite forgotten all about the said son and heir's very existence up till that moment. How is it getting on? I suppose it must quite have forgotten my existence, too, by this time. You forgot to say what the number of its toes and fingers are, explicit as you seem with regard to other particulars; but, I suppose they are the same as usual. Still, I cannot help wondering at so unnatural an instance of inadvertence on your part—not to use a stronger expression. Are its eyes quite as blue as when I saw them last? . . .

*P.S.*—Papa is very much better to-day, and has been writing hard at his lecture since Saturday morning. Mamma seems all right again for the present: both send their best love to you.

*P.P.S.*—It has just struck me that the best way to bring your son and heir would be in a *band-box*, if you come as you promised. The interstices would require to be stuffed up with cotton-wool, and you would be obliged to *cord* the package well to prevent its inmate from knocking the top off, of course. Only, if you *do* this, you had better not let the porters lay hands on it, and it would perhaps be best to take it *into* the cab with you instead of placing it on the *outside*.'

In March Oliver received an invitation to visit Dante Rossetti at Kelmscott, couched in the following terms:—

'*Saturday.*

My dear Nolly,

I am writing Hüffer, asking him to come down next Saturday. He seemed to think a Saturday to Monday visit would suit him best at present, pending the time when he might come with Cathy for a longer stay. Would you accompany him next Saturday to stay a week with us here? And do you think you could get your father to come with you? Perhaps it really might be good for him. There are no floods at present, and though everything is looking bleakish just now, I dare say a week may bring improvement. Give him my love, and say how *very* glad I should be if he could come. *You* at any rate I will hope to see, and when I know I may expect Hüffer and yourself, I will send word to one or other about trains. When you come, bring your work and let us hear it. I heard you had been poetizing as well as novel-writing.

Ever yours,<br>D. G. Rossetti.'

Of the poetizing referred to—evidently *To All Eternity*—some specimens have already been cited, whilst the following irregular but beautiful production, apparently of the same period, is simply entitled

**STANZAS.**

'Oh, delicious sweetness which lingers
  Over the fond lips of love!
Hair-tendrils clinging to fingers
  Tangled in blossom above!
Intense eyes which burn with a light made
  No man knows whereof!
Sweet lips grown more subtle than nightshade,
  More soft than plumes of a dove!

'But love, like a fleet dream eluding
    The desire of a wakening sleeper,
Love, grown too fondly excluding,
    Consumes the heart deeper and deeper
In a passionate waste of desire!
    Like the flame of a desert which rages,
    Our love shall extend through the ages
Though our souls blow asunder like fire.

'Oh, reluctantly lingering breath!
    Oh, longing with sorrow requited!
    Oh, blossom the storm-winds have blighted
Deep down in the shadow of death!'

Anyone bearing such offerings in his hands as this, was certain of a welcome at Kelmscott whilst Dante Rossetti was there. Rossetti was living near Lechlade in an old manor-house which he rented jointly at that time with Mr. William Morris, the poet, who was not, however, a resident then. Kelmscott has been described to us as an ancient, grey stone mansion, with grey stone roofs flecked with black and yellow lichens. Fundamentally, its architecture was of that Tudor style which for some centuries pervaded English country residences, but the upper portion of the building showed signs of a transition to Jacobean, the result either of alterations or more recent additions. The interior was, if somewhat roughly, picturesquely furnished by Rossetti and Morris. Two rooms, one tapestried and the other a wainscoted chamber of the

Jacobean period, were used by Rossetti as studios, and charmingly appropriate studios they must have been for the painter-poet.

The house at Lechlade, and its beautiful old garden enclosed by walls, with a few picturesque trees about it, stood on a gentle knoll, just sufficiently elevated to be high and dry above the Thames floods, which, however, at certain seasons would surround the dwelling. A small channel brought a boat right up to the boathouse from the river. Every convenience of a country residence, stables, kennels, yards, orchards, and so forth, was attached to the place. A small pony Mr. Morris had brought from Iceland, and a number of beautiful dogs belonging to Mr. George Hake, who was then residing with Rossetti, were among the inhabitants. Mr. Hake's celebrated black-and-tan terrier, 'Dizzy,' was one of the guests, and always had a plate provided for him at dinner, dining like the rest of the company, and keeping proudly aloof from the great plebeian out-of-door dogs.

The whole place was exquisitely beautiful, romantic, and thoroughly adapted to the highly susceptible imagination of a youth of Oliver's temperament, whilst the culture and originality of his companions, much older though they were than he in years, were highly delightful, and kept him from regretting London society. Near by the river flowed away through reed and rush and flower-bordered meadows, whilst somewhat further distant stood a fantastic footbridge, leading to a row of desolate cottages which were frequently, in flood time, half under water.

Writing to his father from Kelmscott, on a certain Monday in March, Oliver says:

'DEAR PAPA,

I am sorry not to have written to you long before this, but until Hüffer went this morning I really have not had a moment to myself. It rained so hard the afternoon of the day we started, that we were forced to come straight on here; but with a few exceptions we have had very good weather since. Rossetti seems in a wonderfully good temper at present: George says he has not seen him in such high spirits for a long time past. He has had several long discussions with me on the subject of novel writing, from which I see plainly that he has great facility of expression, but that he would be a dangerous preceptor. Thackeray he will hardly hear the name of; George Eliot is vulgarity personified; Balzac is melodramatic in plot, conceited, wishy-washy, and dull. Dumas is the one great and supreme man, the sole descendant of Shakespeare. For the last three evenings he has played cards with Frantz, George, and what they call a " dummy." . . .

I find I am a very good rider, although the pony tries to throw one off every five minutes; as to rowing, I am almost as good as George, and go two or three miles down the river every morning, all by myself. I have a rather bad sore throat at present. . . . I shall be back on Friday night. With best love to mamma and yourself, believe me,

Very affectionately yours,<br>
OLIVER M. BROWN.'

Instead of returning on the Friday, as promised in his interesting communication, Oliver wrote home on that day,

'DEAR PAPA,

Thank you very much for your card. George has gone to London on some business. Rossetti has asked me particularly to stop till he comes back. He is not expected here before Saturday evening, so I shall return Sunday instead of to-day. I am very glad indeed to hear you are going so soon.

Most affectionately yours,<br>
O. M. B.'

During the interim between the time this letter was written and Oliver's return home, an incident occurred of no slight interest in the even tenor of his uneventful life. As his letter of Monday shows, whilst at Kelmscott, he indulged daily in boating. One afternoon, probably his last in the place, he was absent so long that Dante Rossetti, who was at that time in a state of extreme nervous excitement, grew quite terrified with suspense, picturing all kinds of horrors as having happened to his youthful guest. He paced up and down the rooms, leaving his dinner untouched, and, as he did not dine till ten at that time, it *must* have been late. When at last the truant appeared, Rossetti broke into reproaches, telling the youth that he was responsible to his father for his safety, that he had suffered agonies on his account, that he had pictured his corpse in the ooze of the river, and that he ought to write and tell Mr. Madox Brown the whole affair. Oliver, who at home was indulged with a latch-key, and allowed to come in at any hour of the night without a question being asked, was somewhat at a loss to comprehend his host's excitement. Taking matters very coolly, he merely said, 'I am very hungry, and should like something to eat!'

For the rest of Oliver's stay matters seem

to have quieted down, but after his departure the boat was found to have been damaged, and, apparently, a book belonging to Rossetti to have also suffered hurt or loss. The poet sent a letter upbraiding the youth with his enormities, who, on the receipt of it, was terribly alarmed in his inexperience of such matters, evidently deeming the old boat's repairs would cost nothing less than a hundred pounds or so. Rossetti was not, of course, concerned about the cost of the boat, but about the possible horror of having had to communicate the youth's death by drowning or some other calamity to his parents. Oliver was equally distressed at the idea of his father's being written to, in his usual imaginative way, exaggerating the cost of the damage and his own impecuniosity; the fact being that his father allowed him a pound weekly for dress and pocket money, but that the moment he received any cash he spent it in books. His reply to Rossetti, evidently sent off in hot haste, is most characteristic:

'37, Fitzroy Square, W.,
*Thursday.*

DEAR MR. ROSSETTI,—

I cannot tell you how perturbed I am to have received your last letter, or how bitterly disgusted I am with myself to think that any of my actions during my short stay with you should have deserved it. One thing, however, I can assure you solemnly, on my honour as a gentleman, which is that I knew nothing (as your letter seems to hint) of there being anything wrong with the boat when I arrived at Radcot. I am quite ignorant of all boating matters—I went too far down the stream, and only managed to pull back with the greatest difficulty. When I reached the spot where the boat was left, I was utterly exhausted; it was drizzling with rain; the fog was rising everywhere, and it had grown quite dark: in short, I dared not come further up the stream by myself, and there was nothing to be done but to stop. The man promised it (the boat) should be safe, and I got out. I had on at the moment only a small overcoat with one pocket to it, which was already stuffed up, so I asked him to take care of the book as well, which he also promised to do. How he came to leave it in the boat I can't tell. I do hope and trust you will not tell my father anything about the matter; I have already such a bad character with him, and have done so many things which (God knows!) I ought not to have done, that I fear he would take a positive dislike to me if you did. I hope also the charge for mending the boat will not come to very much; I have not a farthing of money at present, and I fear that (owing to the non-success of my book in a pecuniary point of view), I may be prevented from obtaining any more for my work for some little time to come; but I promise to pay you the moment I can get any.

   I am, dear Mr. Rossetti,
     Yours very faithfully,
        O. M. B.'

In the period between the writing of this letter and the time within which he could receive a reply, Oliver's imagination doubtless conjured up all kinds of horrors in connection with the heavy debt he deemed he had incurred; but the receipt of Rossetti's reply must have at once removed the imaginary incubus from off the lad's mind:

'My dear Nolly,

  To preach to you is one thing (and that was only on the spur of the moment), but to peach to your dad would be quite another thing, and no moment will spur me to that fiendish act.

The photos have just returned here. I was relieved to learn that the thing at the sale is only a replica. Will you let me have your father's address at Cardiff, as I want to write him a word about Llandaff.

Of course no assaults will be made on your purse. The boat may perhaps be exchanged, as it has seen service. If you are needing funds, and like to sell the unfinished picture by . . . . I will give £20 for it almost immediately—not just at this moment, but in a few weeks' time.

Ever yours,<br>D. G. R.

Mind, I don't in the least want to press you to sell the picture if you prefer keeping it, but should like to buy it if you are willing, and am not making the offer merely in case it should be convenient to you.'

Now that his mind was relieved, Oliver's pride was aroused, and he replied:

'37, Fitzroy Square, W.,<br>Monday.

DEAR MR. ROSSETTI,

I am sorry that any careless wording in my last communication should in any way have caused you to look upon it in the light of a begging letter; I have not the slightest necessity for money at present, nor am I at all likely to have any necessity for it. It is only on the very rarest or remotest occasions that I ever dream of spending a farthing. Thank you very much for your offer, however. If you really want the picture mentioned, I should be only too glad that you should accept it as a present, as far as any ownership in it of my own is concerned. Mr. . . . . certainly told me I might have it. (I rather suspect he is hard-up himself at present, in which case he might like you to pay the money to him instead.) Anyhow, if the picture really does belong to me, you shall have it. I will look it up forthwith. With best regards,

Yours most faithfully,<br>
OLIVER MADOX BROWN.

P.S.—You seem under some slight misapprehension with regard to my father's whereabouts. Last Monday he was prevented from starting, and he did not really get off till yesterday evening (Sunday).

I am not as yet aware of his address myself, but the moment I get it, it shall be sent on to you.'

The allusion in the above letter—which like so many of its writer's was wrongly dated—to Mr. . . . . being 'hard-up,' must have been intended by Oliver as irony, as it is scarcely likely that even he, with all his inexperience of pecuniary matters, could have deemed the gentleman alluded to to have been in want of money. Dante Rossetti would seem to have at first declined to receive the painting in question as an unconditional gift, although he still expressed his desire to make it his own. To meet his wishes, Oliver proposed to exchange the portrait for something of Rossetti's own work, to which suggestion came this reply:

'MY DEAR NOLLY,

Thanks for your portrait (not a bad one at all) and for your letter about the picture. My wish to possess the latter is solely as an early portrait of its original, of whom I have made so many studies myself—thus, as long as there is any question of the work becoming mine, please don't touch the figure on any account in the least.

From what you say of the picture, however, it strikes me that I really might not be able with any sort of fairness to meet its value by such exchange as would be in my power, which could merely be represented by some chalk head or other, or something of that sort. I fancy we had better let the subject remain pending till I could see it at your house, but if sent anywhere at present, better to Euston Square, only I don't know when I should be there to look at it.

Ever yours,
D. G. R.'

I am writing Wm. a line on the matter *in case* you do send it to his house.'

Of course Oliver did send it, and as a present, and of course it remained the property of his friend. There is another letter from Rossetti, seemingly written about the same time, referring to another painting, and which is very interesting as evidence of the highly susceptible temperament of the painter-poet:—

'*Thursday.*

DEAR NOLLY,

I am disquieted by the enclosed entry in a catalogue of sale at Christie's for Saturday— whether your father ought to know of it or not. I think you should go to the rooms—King Street, St. James's—and see if it is the original picture of the *Last of England*,\* or only one of the several replicas which I think exist. I fancy the size of the original was larger than fourteen inches diameter, but am not sure. If you thought it necessary, you might telegraph to your father at Cardiff, and he might telegraph to L—— or any probable buyer, who again might telegraph to some one to bid. You will best judge, I suppose. I don't think it worth while unless it

\* One of Mr. Ford Madox Brown's best known paintings.

is the original oil picture—possibly not even then if you think it would bother him too much. I would have sent catalogue before, but only got it last night too late for post, being sent on by hand from Lechlade mid-day post.

Ever yours,<br>D. G. R.'

Some short time earlier than the above correspondence, that is to say, just after Oliver's return from Kelmscott, his interest was aroused for *Music and Moonlight*, the last volume of poetry by Arthur O'Shaughnessy published during its author's lifetime; and moved by that sympathetic feeling which he ever showed for writers whose works he deemed unduly depressed, he wrote to an esteemed friend on its behalf:—

'March 18, 1874.

DEAR MISS BLIND,

O'Shaughnessy's new book is just coming out (as you may perhaps have heard), and I assure you there will be some very powerful poems in it. I should be very sorry to give you any trouble if it were for myself; but could you manage to review it anywhere? I have been greatly disgusted to learn (through Philip Marston) that the copies sent to the . . . . and the . . . . have by some mischance fallen into adverse hands, and are not by any means likely to have justice done them: which (unless some other more favourable review follows) will be quite enough to do for and sink the book. This would be intolerable, for there are many and great beauties in it, with which I am sure you will sympathize. The . . . . was able in a great measure to stop the circulation of my own book by an unfavourable review; but just at present it is all powerful with regard to poetry, and might ruin O'Shaughnessy for good. The Philistines are making such headway nowadays.

At any rate, I hope you will look out for the book and read it. I happened casually to take it up and glance through it, and was instantly struck by the great vivacity and beauty of the verse it contains, and felt indignant that nobody had as yet taken notice of it. It would be a great personal favour to me were you to exert any of the influence you possess in its favour. With best wishes,

Believe me,<br>
Yours always faithfully,<br>
Oliver Madox Brown.'

On the 31st of this month a momentous event happened in the Fitzroy Square household: Miss Lucy Madox Brown, Oliver's elder sister, was married to Mr. William Michael Rossetti, the well-known author. The newly married couple started at once for the Continent, and on the 2nd of April Oliver wrote to the bride in the following terms:

'DEAR LUCY,
    I have just received William's letter, and fear my own will be somewhat late in consequence. We were all very much tired after you left, but papa (up to the present) seems in no degree the worse for it—indeed, as far as I can observe, seems better. I have noticed before that any great excitement or exertion seems to do him good in some way or other, and I think that this rule decidedly holds good at present. He is sorting his letters in the old cabinet—he began them yesterday, but was interrupted by the simultaneous entrance of Swinburne and Miss Blind, who both stopped to dinner.'

Some amusing gossip respecting various literary personages then follows, but, unfortunately, it is of too personal a character for citation here. The youthful correspondent then reverting to his domestic intelligence says:

'Mamma seems also tolerably well at present. I myself had a bad attack of sciatica, or something like it, in the nerves of my left arm, which has gone now, however. Hüffer and Cathy went off to Merton the next day with the infant. Papa and mamma are both going to-night to dine with Miss Blind, to meet Swinburne, Watts, the Bells, and Mr. Stuart Glennie. I am not asked, and am going elsewhere. I went yesterday evening to the . . . ., who are an incredibly queer lot, to say the least of it!

With best wishes to yourself and William,

Ever your affectionate brother,

OLIVER M. BROWN.'

Towards the end of the month, Mr. Madox Brown went to Wales to paint, and thither, on the 2nd of May, his son sent him this letter:

'DEAR PAPA,

We are going on very well up to the present; Cathy left us two days ago. The new housemaid came last night—she is certainly very ugly, indeed, but seems energetic. Late last night I went to meet . . . ., the novelist, who is, to say the least, as commonplace-looking a man as one could meet. . . . . was there too, as bad as he could be, but hugely polite to everyone, and paying outrageous compliments to . . . ., whom, in company with himself, he held up to me as examples of what industrious habits may bring young men of genius to. Poor Mr. . . . . scarcely knew which way to turn, and blushed up to the roots of his hair. He seems very modest, to judge by his talk; all he writes for is to make money, as he said. I can't say that I should care to take him as a preceptor.

Mr. Prange and three other gentlemen called here yesterday: we were out at the time. He wished to know whether you would be back any time this week and of course was told no, at which he expressed regret. A ticket for the private view of the Royal Academy came here Tuesday morning, and was sent to Brookbank immediately, to Manchester. There is no other news whatever. We are going to-night to the Conways', of course. Mamma is going for a few days to Merton on Sunday.

Hoping soon to hear from you,
Ever yours affectionately,
OLIVER MADOX BROWN.'

In connection with this letter to his father at Cardiff, it may be remarked that the card for the

Royal Academy private view, sent off in such hot haste to Manchester, should have been sent to an address in London; indeed, there is too much reason to fear that Oliver's habitual want of care in regard to the common things of life was frequently productive of very tiresome complications.

At this epoch our youthful author spent much of his time in congenial society, both at home and abroad. His company was always in request, people of mature age never appearing to deem it extraordinary, or condescension, to converse with the lad as an equal, and this notwithstanding his *naïveté* and almost childish inexperience on many worldly matters. It is the common remark of his friends that his youth was the last thing one thought of when conversing with him. Although he was most deliberate in utterance, his conversation sparkled with lively and brilliant sayings; but—at least outside his most familiar circle, where he was, as it were, off his guard—was chiefly distinguished for its cynical tone, and it was this, doubtless, that gave him, as has been remarked, the appearance of being older than his father.

In May he was elected member of the Savage Club, and about the same time, if not a member of, he was a frequent visitor at, many other well-known clubs. However, notwithstanding his gregarious inclinations, he still contrived to pursue his linguistic and other studies, as well as keep steadily at work on his literary labours.

Poetry was occasionally essayed, and in a letter of this date to an esteemed friend enclosing a most beautiful lyric, he thus excuses what was naturally an uncontrollable impulse to write verse:

'37, Fitzroy Square, W.

DEAR MISS BLIND,

Should you consider the enclosed worth ten and sixpence or anything whatever, will you forward it and have it printed in the *Examiner*, as you kindly promised? I should not trouble about the matter, were it not that I find myself so long in writing my present novel, that I fear the public may forget all about me again if I don't manage to bring myself in some way to their notice. If you think it puerile (as I dare say it is), throw it in the fire at once: it is one out of some twenty short songs I have been compelled to write (much against my will) for a future novel, *The Dwale Bluth*, of which you heard some portions last year.

With best regards, and in great haste,
Very faithfully yours,
OLIVER MADOX BROWN.'

This 'one out of some twenty short songs' was never included in the romance it was professedly written for, nor has it, indeed, yet been published. It is the most elaborate, if not the most artistic, piece of workmanship in verse that survives of its author, and makes one sigh to think, if the foreshadowing of his poetic career were so sadly sweet, how sweetly grand might not have been the ripeness of his matured manhood. Of the two differing versions of this lyric which are extant, the following is the later :

### BEFORE AND AFTER.

'Ah! long ago since I or thou
Glanced past these moorlands brow to brow,
  Our mixed hair streaming down the wind—
    So fleet! So sweet!
I loved thy footsteps more than thou
Loved my whole soul or body through—
  So sweet! so fleet! ere Fate outgrew the days wherein
  Life sinned!

And ah! the deep steep days of shame,
Whose dread hopes shrivelled ere they came,
  Or vanished down Love's nameless void—
    So dread! so dead!
Dread hope stripped dead from each soul's shame—
Soulless alike for praise or blame—
  Too dead to dread the eternities whose heaven its shame
  destroyed!'

# *THE DWALE BLUTH.*

# From O. M. B.

## AN UNPUBLISHED POEM.

### VII.

Thou shalt not be of those whom Time effaces,
   Whilst yet the mould is moist above their head,
   Whose memories fade and pass, and all is said;
    Nay, for us all who loved thee and who love,
      Shining life's fret above,
Thy thought shall throne it in our hearts' high places,
Till Death blot past and present from our faces;
   Thou shalt not be of the forgotten dead.

   \*     \*     \*     \*     \*     \*

### XI.

And if thy life's untimely ended story—
   Thy life, so thick with many an early bloom
   And seed of blooms far brighter—hold no room,
    For very ratheness, in the inconstant ken
      Of quick-forgetting men,
Yet, for our hearts, though Time himself grow hoary,
The lily of love, if not the rose of glory,
   Shall flower and fade not on thy timeless tomb.

JOHN PAYNE.

*February*, 1883.

## CHAPTER VII.

### *THE DWALE BLUTH.*

AS early as the 27th of September, 1872, Oliver wrote, as has already been said, to Messrs. Smith, Elder and Co.'s reader, that for more than three months he had been engaged on a new romance, a story of Dartmoor and Devonshire country life. 'I intend to name the tale I am now working on,' he wrote, 'either *Deadly Nightshade*, or else to call it by the name of its heroine, *Helen Serpleton*. Although I imagine its style may be said to resemble in some degree that of my first work, yet I think that, as it is much more quiet and dignified, it would stand a better chance of success. I suppose it will make about three volumes. If you do not think *Gabriel Denver* fit to be shown to Messrs. Smith and Elder, would you kindly allow me in a short while to submit to you the first four or five chapters of my new story?'

That Mr. Smith Williams did think *Gabriel Denver* fit to be shown to Messrs. Smith, Elder and Co., is already known, as is also its fate; but probably the instance is unique in literature of a young and quite unknown author deliberately proposing to forego the projected publication of his first novel in order that a second, 'more quiet and dignified,' but as yet unwritten, may be proffered in its stead. The publisher's reader, well satisfied as to the reality of his young correspondent's genius, certainly encouraged him not to remain contented with his initial effort, but to persevere, for the following letter was sent to Mr. Smith Williams on the 15th of November :

'My dear Sir,

I will certainly finish my story as thoroughly and well as I can, and have no doubt that within the next four or five months, at the latest, it will be ready to submit to you. At the risk of troubling you too much, I should be very glad to have your own personal opinion on the chapters which are now in progress. Should you at any time have leisure enough to read them, I could bring them to your office. It is very easy to alter faults while one is at work: but it becomes a difficult and troublesome thing to alter work which has been once set aside as finished, even though the defects pointed out are perfectly recognisable. But at present there is scarcely a third of the story written.

As you do not seem to consider *Deadly Nightshade* a good name, I have thought of calling it *Nightshade* alone. Should this not suit, it might still be called *The Dwale Bluth*—which is an old North Devonshire word for the plant. This could at any rate have nothing repulsive about it—and being original, and somewhat mysterious as well, it might possess a certain interest. I at first intended to call the tale *Belladonna*, a title which would have been very applicable and suggestive; but a friend informed me that there was already a novel with that name, so it was out of the question. I might still call it by the scientific name, *Atropa Belladonna*. However, there is no very great necessity to decide upon this point at present, though I should like to settle it.

Believe me, dear sir,
Very faithfully yours,
OLIVER MADOX BROWN.'

The life Oliver now led did not allow him much leisure for his literary labours. His studies naturally absorbed some portion of his time, whilst a still larger section of it was taken up with visiting and being visited; nor was his health good, terrible headaches and, as has been seen, other ailments making frequent chasms in the few precious hours that remained. All things considered, it is not, therefore, surprising to find him writing to Mr. Williams on the 24th of December in such terms as these: 'I have not been working at my story during the last four weeks; and, indeed, have had very little time for anything. Before setting to work on it again, I shall take the liberty of calling upon you, and—if you could spare the time—of informing you of a project I have thought of for rewriting the first story I submitted to you.' That the project of rewriting *Gabriel Denver* was carried out, although in a very different way to what the author designed, has already been explained. Two months or so were wasted in the mutilation of the unfortunate *Gabriel Denver*, or rather its progenitor, *The Black Swan*, at the end of which period Oliver's thoughts were diverted in another direction, the result of which was so much of *Hebditch's Legacy* as remains to us.

Ultimately Oliver returned to his old love, and recommenced work on *The Dwale Bluth*, a fact which towards the end of July, 1874, he communicated to Messrs. Smith, Elder and Co.'s reader in the following very characteristic manner:

'You may perhaps have expected to see or hear from me again before now, after the kind spirit in which you took up my last book. I have, however, felt disinclined to encroach on your valuable time without good reason, or some work near enough completion to show you, which I have not as yet. I have, indeed, begun and carried considerably forward three novels within the last nine months; but the one I have decided to go on with for the present is a rather long story, of which only some twenty-two chapters are written; but which cannot possibly be finished before the close of the year, if even then. . . . I shall in any case be glad to hear from you. . . .

OLIVER MADOX BROWN.'

In response to the young author's communication, Mr. Smith Williams expressed his pleasure at hearing that another novel was in progress, and hoped 'the subject may be more agreeable than the first, for people read novels,' he opined, 'to be amused, and have surfeited on painful stories; in short, the public has "supped full of horrors." If it should be a two-volume book,' said Mr. Williams, 'so much the better; single volumes do not pay, and people are rather tired of three-volume novels. I hope you will take your time over your new fiction, by only writing when in the vein, which is the only surety for real good work. Feeling a strong interest in your new work, I must confess to a wish to know something of it, though from curiosity only.'

A few days later, on the 4th of August, Mr. Williams wrote to Oliver: 'I take the earliest opportunity of telling you that there may be an opening in the *Cornhill Magazine* by the time you have finished your story,' and added, 'if you can spare what is written of the MS. I shall be happy to submit it to the editor at once before he leaves town.'

Warned by the treatment his first romance had received at the hands of the *Cornhill* editor, Oliver's pride did not permit him to feel greatly elated at the prize dangled before his eyes by the kindly reader, to whom he replied on the 5th of August:

'My dear Sir,

I feel much gratified by both the kind letters you have written me; I was just about to reply to the first when the second one came, and caused me again to defer answering, as I had to consider your valued suggestion.

You may not have heard yourself what I have been told on excellent authority—that the editor of the *Cornhill* is the writer of the notice referred to in my last letter on *Gabriel Denver*, in the *Saturday Review;* but I think you will agree with me, seeing this to be the case, that I have very good reason for not again wishing to offer any work of my own to that magazine. To yourself, however, you must probably be well aware (both from our previous correspondence and from your last letter to me), that I shall have the greatest pleasure in showing my manuscript in due time, should no at present unforeseen circumstance deter its completion: and you may be certain that should the nature of my future writings permit, I would much rather publish them under your auspices than with any other house. . . . I shall ever remain with sincerity, my dear sir,

   Yours very faithfully,
    Oliver Madox Brown.'

The friendly feelings Mr. Smith Williams had grown to entertain for his youthful correspondent, and the firm belief he had in his genius, would not allow him to let slip the fancied opening for his romance; he, therefore, upon receipt of Oliver's reply, wrote to him: 'Without questioning your authority, I venture to doubt the fact you mention. But be it as it may, I would strongly recommend you to *let me show* your MS. to the editor of the *Cornhill Magazine;* and when I tell you that he was inclined to accept *Gabriel Denver*, I hope you will not object. I may mention,' added Mr. Williams in a *postscript*, 'that my showing the MS. will not implicate you in any way; but I don't want to let this opportunity slip.'

Persuaded, if not convinced, Oliver gave his consent; and ultimately altered the plan of his projected romance, in order to suit it to the requirements of the *Cornhill* editor. After having the story under revision for some time, he wrote the following letter to Mr. Williams:

'My dear Sir,—

I have delayed sending you the accompanying chapter until now, in order to finish the eighth, which, I think, is rather an important one. In reading it you will doubtless notice that (in compliance with Mr. Stephen's remark), I have attempted to bring Helen Serpleton more forward, and have, also, completely modified the country dialect. I shall in a few days have finished the third part.

I have done nothing as yet to preceding chapters, and should very much like to have your opinion on them—although I hope you will not put yourself to inconvenience by looking over them until you can thoroughly spare the necessary time.

Believe me, dear sir,<br>Very faithfully yours,<br>OLIVER MADOX BROWN.'

As will thus be seen, the same heart-breaking system of mutilation and alteration that had sufficed to injure *The Black Swan* was now at work to destroy the vitality of *The Dwale Bluth*. In order to satisfy the suggestions of the magazine editor, as he had had formerly to give way to the publisher's reader, Oliver now deviated from the plan originally laid down for his story, a story even finer in many respects than his initial romance, and one that, had it ever been completed, would alone have won its author an extensive and all-enduring reputation. As it is, *The Dwale Bluth* is such a grand fragment in prose as is the *Hyperion* of Keats in poetry, and while the magnificent torso Keats left half-hewn was the production of a man of twenty-five, the wonderful fabric Oliver left unfinished was the work of a lad but little over nineteen!

After the revised manuscript of the earlier chapters had been retained by the editor of the *Cornhill Magazine* for some time, it was *sent back* to Oliver *without a word!* Deferring for the present any allusion to the injurious effects this proceeding exercised upon the poor lad's highly sensitive temperament, let us advert to the story of *The Dwale Bluth* itself.

'The moment that we begin the first chapter,' says an appreciative critic in reviewing the *Literary Remains* of Oliver Madox Brown,[*] 'we perceive that the author has got into a new world. We perceive that he has taken a leap from the realm of exaggeration and riotous exercise of lawless power, to the world of truth and beauty where alone art can live—a leap such, perhaps, as no young writer ever took so suddenly before. We perceive, too, that *we*, on our part, have come upon something new—upon a kind of precocity that is very likely unique, in our country at least. . . . That the work of

[*] The *Examiner*, January 29, 1876.

youth should ever be otherwise than crude and acrid is wonderful, indeed. Still more wonderful is it if the humour of youth is anything more than exaggeration, caricature, phantasy. "Humour is always a late growth," says Barry Cornwall in regard to Lamb. But in *The Dwale Bluth* we get humour—humour which is philosophic, at once, and dramatic—humour which unquestionably affines the writer to the great prose humourists. If the highest humour is that which is at the same time truthful representation, the greatest humourist of our century is George Eliot. Yet there are scenes in *The Dwale Bluth*, which, though not equal to hers, may be compared with them.'

*The Dwale Bluth* is a Devonian name for 'Deadly Nightshade'—a blossom which literally, as well as symbolically, plays an important part in the story—and signifies 'Frenzy-flower,' or 'Craze-bloom.' But the romance, its appropriate title notwithstanding, concerns the fortunes of the Serpleton family, and more particularly Helen, the last representative of the ruined race. The scions of this family were ever wayward and graceless, and in some occult manner were connected with the Tracys, the ancestor of whom was ringleader in the martyrdom of Thomas à Becket, and consequently, transmitter to his descendants of the curse laid on the murderers and his progeny; for, says the ballad:

> 'Woe to the unborn sons of the Tracys!
> (*Say what redemption is left through all time*)
> O could they reach to the land where God's grace is,
> Baffled and faint with the storm-wind's embraces—
> (*The wind that wails for their forefather's crime*)
> With ever the wind and rain in their faces—
> Never again till the end of time.'

In the introductory chapter to the romance, a rapid survey of the fortunes of the Serpleton family in more modern times, shows that if some members did not succeed in purging themselves from ancestral sin by attaining the Holy Land, they contrived to have an extremely lively time of it in their own country, notwithstanding the barometrical malediction they lay under. The unobtrusive but suggestive way in which this hereditary curse is seen from time to time overtaking the members of the afflicted race is most artistically wrought into the texture of the story, and certainly equals, if it resemble, the mannerism of Hawthorne. The critic just quoted, as evidence of Oliver's humouristic power, cites the following scene from the history of the Serpletons:

'Sir Geoffrey, the third baronet, then lived till near sixty, though they called him the hardest drinker for nearly twenty miles around, which was saying something at that time, and truly, for the last five years of his existence he is affirmed only *once* to have been found sober after nightfall.

'On this memorable occasion it would appear that old Sir Geoffrey Serpleton and a party of sworn friends met together one Christmastide, in the year of our Lord 1727, with a firm intention of enjoying themselves after their own fashion; and ere they parted, many were the songs whose choruses the walls of Serpleton House echoed under that night; riotous old love or hunting catches, more or less melodious, long-lost or forgotten; and many were the jests they broke between them. Never had Sir Geoffrey seemed in better spirits, jovial-hearted as he ever was; you could have heard him out on the hills round Watern Tor. Anyhow, the carouse of these doughty topers was prolonged through the night to an early hour the next morning. But at last Mrs. Drusilla Hibbledeen, the baronet's housekeeper, rousing from her slumbers at the customary hour, found it still dark, and not wishing to waste candle-light, determined to lie quiet in her bed a few minutes longer.

'Half awake and half asleep, she listened drowsily to the din and confusion overhead.

'Presently, just as she was dropping off to

sleep again, she was called to mind by one of the revellers above, who slid helplessly from his chair, shaking the floor and rattling the windows sharply in their sashes.

' It was a familiar sound enough to her.

' *On her wrinkled finger-joints, she in the course of half an hour had added eleven other thuds to that*, as the guests, following their friend's example, gave way one after another and rolled promiscuously under her master's hospitable board.

' *But there was a thirteenth to the party, and she lay a long while listening for him too.* Nothing happened, however; his wits had given in before she woke, seemingly.

'. Then, throwing off her nightcap, and with her teeth chattering (just as the yellow dawn broke vaguely among the frost-bitten clouds in the east), she got out of bed; preparing, as was her wont, to set to rights the room in which they all lay—to move a leg or an arm here and there, or loosen a cravat. The door was not easy to open, however, for one of the inmates had fallen against it. At last she affected an entrance, and glanced round her. . . . A cheerless frosty sunbeam, streaming in through the half-opened shutters, had fallen full on the puckered face and gray hairs of Sir Geoffrey Serpleton, the baronet, who still sat bolt upright in his chair, grasping a glass, half-filled, and with its stem knocked off. His eyes stared straight in front of him with a ghastly unaverted look—his features were convulsed but motionless—his arms and hands were rigid. The fire had long gone out; but two or three of the candles still guttered in their sockets. These, with the pallid resplendence of the sunbeam, enabled the old servant to perceive *the warm breath issuing from the open lips and nostrils of her master's comrades*—not to mention other tokens given forth among them; but there was no perceptible sense of vitality on Sir Geoffrey's own lips. And, indeed, terrified as she was, she saw in an instant how her master was in a condition of sobriety destined never again to be disturbed.

' It seemed, from the expression of his face, as though the sunlight had reached him ere he was quite dead, and he had been striving helplessly to shut his paralyzed eyelids, or to avoid it in some way.

' The first of the party that regained sufficient sensibility to articulate plainly, is said to have been, of all men in the world, the parish clergyman! There was, however, an utter blank in his memory, save that he recollected noting the ominous number who sat down the day before, at which Sir Geoffrey burst into wild laughter, to the dismay of all present for a time, until they had forgotten it again. And as to the others, put out of countenance, as one may expect them to have been, they remembered nothing whatsoever.'

'This scene,' remarks the reviewer, 'so full of humour, yet so self-restrained, so full of dramatic life and philosophic observation, was written by a boy of eighteen. And note the close observation, the brief and rapid selection of physiognomic details in the words italicized by us. Here we have another characteristic, too, that is almost never seen in so young a writer. The impetuous imagination of youth—seeing its images hanging, as it were, in the air—leaps towards its realization of them, scorning details, and too impatient to take care, save for broad and general effects. Accuracy of detail comes afterwards, comes of that loving outlook upon the world which is born of greatly living in it, enjoying greatly, and greatly suffering.'

Deservedly high as the reviewer praises the scene just cited, it is certain that many other extracts might be made from *The Dwale Bluth* of still greater excellence. For instance, the description of the death of the fourth baronet, Sir Jasper, and his burial—after no little delay and inconvenience—is drawn by a most masterful hand, and with an amazing power of local colour, fully bearing out the critic's assertion, 'you seem to be breathing Devonshire air.' When this baronet's death took place, his elder son [another Jeffery, like his grandfather a notorious 'blind-blossom,' and a fit representative of the restless, wayward, and eccentric characteristics of his race] was rambling in unknown parts, but ultimately, and when least expected, returned, in company with a young woman, apparently of gipsy origin, whom he had picked up somewhere in Spain, and 'married at first sight.'

The only person who appeared to be in any way interested in the baronet's return was old Margery—grand-daughter of the Mrs. Hibbledeen above named—to whom Serpleton House had so long been left in undisturbed possession, that to have to relinquish the command to a mistress—and she an uncomprehended foreigner —was a terrible blow. Many were the attempts she made to express her indignation to the master's wife, but in vain, as were also her repeated attempts to make out what she talked to her husband about. 'In the privacy of the back kitchen (where long seclusion had given Margery a habit of holding conversation with herself), she would express her opinion with astonishing volubility concerning the wild "outlandisher," as she called her mistress. Then, when in a more than usually bitter frame of mind, she would sweep the floor, worry the saucepans, shake her well-fed cat out of its favourite chair, and even fling dish-clouts or saucepan-lids after the astonished animal, till it must have thought its mistress had taken leave of her senses.'

After a while a baby was born, and 'even Margery was moved by the devotion Dolores displayed for the offspring. Many were the recipes and remedies she longed vainly to bestow upon the devoted baby; at the slightest manifestation of blackness in the face, or the faintest symptoms of rigidity about the toes and fingers, her anxiety would become dreadful to contemplate;' but of course, as neither understood the other's language, no verbal communication was possible. 'Helen had the sweetest little hands and feet; they were so small that the fond mother could place them in her own mouth, though the baby was usually employed performing this service for herself; now and then, aided by her soft gums, she seemed to be making long and careful calculations as to the actual amount of fingers and toes she really possessed, but it was a difficult and problematical point, if one could have judged by the frown which dimpled her wide brows at such intervals.' Another little picture of baby-life is presented, where the mother is seen carrying Helen downstairs one night, when the yellow flickering candlelight 'fell upon its little face, in which even now a promise of future health and beauty was visible. Its mouth was clasping her bosom, and its little tender hands were seen pushing out energetically, just in the way one sometimes notices a suckled kitten forcing a larger supply of nutriment with its forepaws.'

But, however naturally infant life and animal life are portrayed in *The Dwale Bluth*, it is in his grasp of character and clever delineation of individuality that Oliver manifests his great power. Old Margery, with her crusty temper and strong Devonian dialect, is a wonderful portraiture, and in her shrewdness and sarcastic repartee would have been a match for Mrs. Poyser herself. Indeed, the keen sense of humour and quick perception of the ridiculous which Oliver shows in this romance are, all things considered, his most marvellous traits, and those least to be expected in so youthful an author. The whole episode of the robbery of the chicken-house by the gipsies, the rescue of the solitary survivor, and the repaying the outraged Margery with fowls stolen from some one else, is an unsurpassed piece of humouristic fiction.

The old housekeeper's discussions with the various personages of the story are most characteristic, and her biting sarcasm always ready. The old woman was especially wrathful with the servant of the late Mrs. Oliver Serpleton, Jenny, who for some months after her mistress's death remained a member of the household, till she was expelled for insubordination. Margery, alarmed at the maid's 'squanderous' ways, had taken her thoroughly to task in a speech full of Devonshire vituperation and insinuation.

'This tirade naturally provoked Jenny into retorting that she was 'quite good enoo' for Margery,' she being 'just as the Lord had chuzzin ter mek her, naught else!' 'More's th' pity!' quoth Margery sorrowfully. 'A' must a' been cruel hard up fer summat ter dew th' marn; squandering a's hendywerk on a frizzle-de-Morndy loik ter thicker!'

The story can scarcely be deemed to commence, however, until Jeffery departs with his wife and baby, and leaves the old place to the occupation of his brother, the Rev. Oliver Serpleton, and his *ménage*. Oliver Serpleton is assuredly, his creator's masterpiece: his eccentricities are so lovingly displayed and his various idiosyncrasies so shrewdly described, that we seem to know the man thoroughly and, despite his peculiarities, like him or at any rate sympathize with him heartily. Even his apparent insensibility at his poor wife's death is only, *as we know*, in seeming, and at the bottom of his heart there is a deep reservoir of kindness and humanity. For, as our author says when referring to Mr. Serpleton's supposed indifference, 'It is sometimes awful to think how little we really are capable of fathoming the minds of the very people who are nearest and dearest to us; and seeing this is the case, it is easy to understand the way our actions are misinterpreted by strangers.'

The simplicity and good-nature of the exclergyman are admirably portrayed by such typical little verbal vignettes as is this account of the persecution he endures at the instance of a kitten of too exuberant spirits:—

'Mr. Serpleton's favourite place of study consisted of the landing-stage outside his bedroom, where there was a settle fixed under the window: there he would sit absorbed for hours in the contemplation of some old mouldy volume or other. It was here that Margery once found him, remonstrating feebly and ineffectually with a sportively-inclined kitten, which, having knocked the book out of his hands, had not been content thereat, but had mounted on the window-sill, and thence had maintained a fierce and unintermittent warfare on the black ribbons of his queue. Then this feline imp proceeded to clasp him round the neck with her soft fore-paws, and to go through many wonderful gymnastic evolutions on his shoulders, until, with the old servant's assistance, it was dislodged, only to return to the assault when she was gone. In fact, the poor man fell a martyr to this animal, and always promptly disappeared when it met his view. But at last the animal grew up, became more grave in demeanour, and left him in peace.'

Mr. Serpleton's introduction to his own daughter Leah when she was three years old is another amusing and naturally told incident; but a still more important matter, so far as the plot and interest of the romance are concerned, is that of his first interview with his niece Helen, when her father Jeffrey, meeting the clergyman, informs him of his wife's death, and leaves his only child in his brother's charge. Helen, when introduced to Uncle Nolly, was about five or six years old, and at the interview is described as a little girl ' whose acute eyes seemed to sparkle even in the darkness. Her hair (which was so black as to form a still blacker spot in the obscurity of the night) was filled with a most extraordinary display of moving lights; in fact, a multitude of living glow-worms were crawling about in it.' Left in Mr. Serpleton's charge, little Helen, the heroine of the book, 'clasped her uncle's hand with her own icily cold little fingers (for the unreasoning desire to hold a "grown-up's" hand amounts to an instinct in all children),' and went home to her new and unknown abode. How scandalized Margery was at receiving this unexpected and unprovided-for charge, and how tormented she was by the hapless glow-worms, must be gathered from *The Dwale Bluth* itself.

The second book of the romance opens with a charming, realistic account of Serpleton House, followed by a description of the inmates. Helen's childish beauty inspires such thoughts as these: 'A child's face resembles an unexpanded bud. As a thinker examines the undeveloped promise of the coming blossom, he sees the remote future lying before it: filled, may be, with the vague ineffable luxuriousness of the dream which beauty weaves around itself, but also pregnant with the old and shadowy threatenings of sorrow and decay. . . . There is something very sorrowful in the sight of a human being so utterly unaware of what things life may have one day in store for it.' The half-gipsy child in her rambles about the precincts of Serpleton House has a companion, which Oliver, from his intimate acquaintance with domestic animal life, is enabled to characteristically depict. 'She was accompanied,' he says, 'by a weird-looking grey cat, just emerging from kittenhood, not yet grown dignified or lazy enough to be capable of resisting such allurements as were presented to its youthful feline nature by chasing and capturing the quick grasshoppers, or the gilded flies buzzing over the grass and in and out of the speckled sunshine.' Sometimes the kitten, which singularly resembled its little mistress in many respects, did not succeed in capturing its prey; 'after these failures the animal, writhing in and out of the girl's feet, while she stood still, seemed to talk and purr as though it were convinced its mistress understood its inarticulate language, and was probably endeavouring to encourage her to fresh exertions.' And thus the pretty picture of the two youthful comrades proceeds, showing its author's most familiar knowledge of both child and animal life.

Little Helen Serpleton has not forgotten the Zingali teachings of her mother, and sings such little snatches of song in the Spanish gipsy dialect as this:

> 'I love very well
>   The first blossoming
> (I love well I ween)
>   That blooms in the spring;
> Its purple and green
> Seem meet for some queen,
>   To bind in her hair's loosening.
>
> '"I should love well to match me!
>   (The light of high heaven
> Burns in my eyes!)
>   And I love well," she cries,
> "The young men to watch me.
> But, ah! who can catch me?
> For I run with feet fleeter than wind through the skies."'

A theory of Oliver Madox Brown, but by no means peculiar to him, is thus succinctly propounded for him by Philip Bourke Marston, in his *Lament* for his friend:

> 'I know it was of his a favourite creed
>   That when the body dies the existing soul
> Of other souls becomes a fruitful seed,
>   Changing, existing through the years that roll';

and amid the curious reflections suggested to the young author's mind by the thought of the many generations of singers through whom the Zingali songs had been transmitted, he does not fail to refer to this theory. Thus he says:

'Those gracious lips, burnt red by the sun, which had first learnt to pronounce them in the sultry splendour of the eastern climes they had issued from, had long since been silenced; even the very dust the limbs of the singers had dissolved into must have perished and been drawn up and reinhaled into fresh flesh and blood, which had itself perished again. The disused vital forces of their souls might even now be suffused among the gusts of wind which blew about the unconscious child's tangles of hair; for it was one of those songs which are handed down through remote long centuries from generation to generation; dying away from echo to echo fainter and fainter, as it were a voice among the mountains. There is nothing more saddening than the pleasure given by an old melody; one knows not what long-passionless hearts may once have been inspired with rapture over its still undiminished sweetness; but indeed there are very few things in this world which are utterly unmingled with any suggestion of the final mystery of our existences.'

But such psychological speculations are not so frequent in *The Dwale Bluth* as in their author's initial romance; in the later work his strength being chiefly displayed in the portrayal of character more by its outer and visible, than its inner and hidden idiosyncrasies. A characteristic and life-like scene is that between Oliver Serpleton, his daughter Leah, and niece Helen, wherein the Deadly Nightshade, the ill-omened plant after which the book is named, makes its first appearance in the story. Attracted by the strange blossom and glittering berries of a spray of *The Dwale Bluth*, the two girls had had a scramble for it, and Leah was the successful one, yet scarcely had clasped it ere her cousin Helen snatched the prize out of her hand. Mr. Serpleton being appealed to, took the spray, and after examination pronounced it to be the dreaded and dangerous *atropa belladonna*. ' " Look here, Nelly, and you, too, Leah," he said, " they call this the deadly nightshade sometimes. You must never disturb it, or it will send you to sleep so soundly that you won't be able to wake up again. It's poison, mark you!"

' Leah shuddered childishly, and seemed to recede from the place where she plucked it, rubbing her small hands and fingers on her frock. Helen, who had remained silent during this slowly and painfully delivered dialogue, merely looked with deep curiosity on the leaves which hung out of the pocket he had placed the plant in when he had ceased speaking. Had he thrown it away at once, as he should have done, much of this narrative would have remained unwritten.

'Apparently out of bravado, the child stretched out her ten fingers (which, by-the-bye, were not over-clean already), and touched the leaves with them, and then, having contaminated them sufficiently, put them all to her dark-red lips. What her object could be was inconceivable.

'Leah merely nodded her head, and remarked with more real penetration than one would have expected from her (though children among themselves realize each other's dispositions far better than we can), "Ay! ay! it's th' very daps o' tha'!"'*

Naturally all the originality and truthful aspect of such a scene is lost when torn from its surroundings: to comprehend its force and beauty one must know and appreciate the characters of the absent-minded *savant* and the two children, every word and action of the book being stages in the development of our knowledge of them. The wonderful description of the storm which follows speedily after the discovery of the deadly nightshade is a magnificent piece of word-painting, in every respect fit to match the terrible tableau of the ship on fire in *The Black Swan*. This really good picture is too lengthy for ex-

'It's just what one might have expected from you.'

tract in full, occupying as it does nearly two whole chapters, and to mutilate it by abridgment would be sacrilege. Oliver Madox Brown might very contentedly have based his claims to remembrance upon the two rival but complementary pictures so realistically and powerfully drawn in the pages of his chief romances : both so grand and yet so utterly unlike each other.

A very different but thoroughly idiosyncratic scene is that following the storm, and describing Helen's reception by old Margery when the truant comes home wet and draggletailed from the mist and rain, whilst the incident of her feline friend's return is described with Oliver's usual intimate and sympathetic knowledge of animal life. The drenched child was holding the kitten in her arms, out of which it jumped suddenly as Helen approached the house, sprang into the doorway, ' and in spite of the zealous efforts made by the old servant to frustrate its " dampingness," made good its way on to the polished reflecting tiles of the passage. A dripping trail of moisture betrayed every place in which it set its feet the whole way through the basement of the house, till it reached and crouched down panting on the clean white hearth, in front of the kitchen fire, diffusing a damp patch of moisture all round it on the absorbing whitening of the stone. The large black cat, its mother, after advancing eagerly to welcome the prodigal, started back in utter dismay at its dismal condition, and discreetly laid aside all present ebullitions of maternal solicitude.'

In the third book of *The Dwale Bluth*, entitled 'The Growth of a Soul,' Helen's friendship for her constant companion, the kitten, is thus commented upon:—

'Now Helen *must* have had some particles of good in her nature, if she were not wholly immaculate, like some heroines, for no one acquainted with the feline disposition could ever believe in the existence of a cat capable of forming an enthusiastic friendship with a person of utterly vitiated and unprincipled morals.

'The child once found this animal in the garden, growling angrily over something which she at first mistook for a stone, but afterwards discovered to be nothing more or less than a large and venerable toad. She had probably never seen or heard of such an animal before.

'At any rate, this delightful beast was immediately rescued and examined with great curiosity; its ridiculous shape, cold skin, and palpitating throat, seemed to have something highly attractive to her, for she laughed over them till she nearly dropped the impassive animal into the claws of the expectant cat. At last she placed it on a large stone and bent over it to watch its movements.

'It turned its clumsy feet and toes in quietly, and then sat upright with equanimity, seemingly quite undisturbed by all it had undergone; but presently it turned its flat head knowingly on one side. A fly was approaching.

'The unconscious fly pursued its zigzag course, its golden scales glistening in the sunlight. Nearer and nearer! Helen's eyes glittered with excitement.

'The toad's cunning gold-rimmed eyes glittered too—a white hungry streak flashed out of its distended mouth. The fly was gone, and its captor seemed undergoing a slight internal convulsion, which required the immediate thrusting of his forepaws down his capacious throat.

'After this he winked in a pleasant and suggestive fashion, which can only be thoroughly appreciated by those who have watched a toad wink. The child thought he was winking right in her face—making, in fact, a sign of approval to her. This enraptured her very soul. After winking he commenced patting his flabby-speckled stomach with both paws, for the unhappy insect was most likely tickling him. Helen grew wild with excitement and enthusiasm. She carried him with her into the kitchen, and the cat followed them, growling with disappointment.

'But to her amazement Margery no sooner saw what she held in her hand than she dropped her broom, threw her apron over her face, screamed, and scurried out of the room.

'So, seeing that her nurse was too narrow-minded to appreciate her last acquisition in the way of the fauna of Watern Tor, she carried the animal up to her uncle's room. Now Helen noticed that *he* was not at all frightened at it; for, on the contrary, he took the poor despised beast up in his hands and bestowed a learned Latin surname upon it.

'"Child," said he, handing it carefully back to her, "what do you mean to do with this animal?"

'"Keep him," said Helen.

'"Very well," answered Mr. Serpleton; "but you must not hurt it, and, perhaps . . . upon the whole you would do best . . . not to show it to Margery. It *does* eat, although I have heard the contrary asserted."

'"He does!" remarked Helen.

'In a short while the animal grew tame enough to delight in having its head and ears tickled with a blade of grass; and its owner did nothing but wander over the house and garden watching for flies almost as intently as it could have done itself.

'But Margery never could be reconciled to its presence, and she even went so far as to complain to her master, though without avail. This offended her sense of dignity; but all she could do in her own defence was to refuse sternly to admit the abomination into her sanctuary, the kitchen. She never went to bed at night without trembling lest she should find the animal somewhere among the blankets. She seemed, indeed, to look upon a toad as a kind of hybrid between a viper and a scorpion.'

*The Dwale Bluth* is replete with such charming little incidents of animal and child life, the result, as numerous allusions prove, of actual observation and experience, and not of mere inference from reading. The introduction into the story of the nightingales is roughly paralleled in some passages already cited from a letter to Philip Bourke Marston, and needs not quotation here; but the happy touches of humour which Oliver loved to mingle, not discordantly, but harmoniously, with the poetry and pathos of his prose, is amusingly illustrated in such an instance as that wherein the account of Helen, rising from her bed to listen in a kind of ecstasy to the birds, 'with her white face pressed against the cold window-panes,' is followed by the remark that 'the cat also would leave the bed, mount the window still, and gaze through the misty glass with an extremely earnest expression, though, probably, it took this trouble from less æsthetical motives.'

If the current of the story runs somewhat sluggishly, at least at first, the reader has no reason to regret it, nor does he find need to 'skip' a single page, so interesting and delightful are the digressions, if such the necessary developments of the character of the persons and places introduced may be termed. The reappearance of the ill-omened deadly nightshade suffices for an event, and, indeed, its second advent is fraught with consequences almost tragical. When Mr. Serpleton had returned home on the day in which he had placed the baneful bloom in his pocket, he found and turned it out on to a table. Margery seized the spray and flung it into the garden, where it fell within the shelter of an old cucumber frame and there took root, and says Oliver, 'prospered, as poisonous weeds will sometimes prosper in this world.'

Some weeks passed by, and Helen had never succeeded in discovering any more blossoms or berries of the fascinating plant, although, it is intimated, she had long sought them. One autumnal day, after a stormy interview with Margery, she found herself cooling her passion in the garden. 'She sat down on the edge of the cucumber-frame, drumming her small feet against the side in an impatient way. . . . Of a sudden she started, and bent over the broken bars. *There* was what she had been looking after, for her downcast eyes fell, with an instantaneous revival of interest, on the tendrils of the deadly nightshade, loaded with poison flowers and berries, crawling stealthily round the inside of the frame, or crouching ignominiously along the damp ground. The traces of snail-tracks went all over the bricks and mould, and the leaves were bitten here and there; but *it was singular to note what a number of empty snail-shells were lying among its foliage.* In spite of this, it had grown into a goodly plant.

'The Dwale Bluth is a cowardly creeper, and knows no means of rising above the earth it springs from, unless by insinuating itself among the leaves of some bolder parasite. There it now lay beneath her gaze, even throwing a grim and sinister reflection on to her dark-complexioned face, and into her eyes; there it lay at her feet, prone and helpless, as though it were entreating her to lift it.'

The result of this unfortunate discovery of the poison flower was that Helen, although aware to some extent of its evil qualities, in her wild rage at having been thwarted by Margery, ate of the malign berries. 'Some two hours afterwards Margery found the child moaning in a strange and pitiful manner. She had gone up to her bedroom and was lying on the bed, with her small brown hands clenched in the counterpane; her eyeballs had grown dark and luminous, but seemed no longer to retain the acute and piercing look which usually distinguished them. Indeed, there was an expression of pain all over her face, and her red curved lips twitched constantly.' The old nurse concluded the child had a sick headache, so undressed her and put her to bed.

When Margery returned in a little while with some lemonade decoction, she was horrified to find Helen suffering from paroxysms of a mysterious kind: her alarm was broken in upon by the entrance of Mr. Serpleton. He quickly perceived that the child was suffering from the effects of poisoning, but for some time could not detect what was the nature of the venom. Eventually he discovered the cause of the evil and administered a suitable draught, and although Margery, who had been despatched for the nearest medical man, had to return without him, she found her master had ably fulfilled the duties of nurse and doctor too. For a long time Helen lay in a state of delirium, the psychological phases of which are wonderfully depicted, but, owing to the terrible gap in this weird, unfinished romance, we have no record of her recovery, nor of those incidents of her girlhood which the author doubtless intended to supply. The end of the third book, so far as it has been published, leaves Helen Serpleton as a child, suffering from the poisonous effects of the deadly nightshade, whilst the opening chapter of the fourth book introduces her as a grown woman— the widowed mistress of Thurlstone—deprived of her uncle, and with a very uncanny reputation amongst her rustic neighbours. How the author would have bridged the chasm can but be guessed at.

The fourth book introduces Helen loitering with her lover, Arthur Haenton, about the rocks overhanging the sea, talking with him of her past, and planning bright schemes for the future. Arthur, whose prototype is so easy to guess at, is both a poet and blind, and Helen sings snatches of his own songs to him as they saunter along in the twilight. Their feet are arrested by voices, and in the nearness they hear, sung by a shrill chorus of childish throats, this simple Devonshire song :—

> ' A dwalin\* drumble-drone† i' th' rewts,
>     An apple-dreane ‡ aboo :
>   Th' yapple-dreane sturtled § an' stugged i' th' freuts,
>     Th' drone i' th' yavil ‖ flew.

> ' An' apple-drene an' a drumble-drone
>     Wert aw' ther' wert ter zee.
>   Th' drumble-drone lay dead i' th' snaw,
>     Th' yapple-dreane i' th' dree.'

The purport of this charming rustic lyric, which breaks in upon the impassioned lovers' talk, is to relate the story of a bee and wasp, one of whom lived in the roots, the other in the branches of an apple-tree, and who, overtaken by a snow-storm, both came to untimely ends. The chatter of the youngsters and their dread of the 'witch,' as they deem Helen to be, is an amusing and realistic picture of pastoral life that serves to set off and deepen the sombreness and gloom of a tragic tale.

Mrs. Thurlstone and her lover passed up towards the Castle Rock overlooking the sea, followed at a very respectable distance by the youngsters, who, however, were soon put to flight by a man they deemed they recognised as

\* Delirious.    † Bee.    ‡ Wasp.
§ Buzzed.        ‖ Common.

the apparition of Mr. Thurlstone, who, it was supposed, had perished abroad. The lovers, unconscious of the danger impending, passed to the lofty summit of a crag overhanging the sea and then on a fallen stone, sat under the shelter of a natural cave formed by large fragments of rock. Thither the returned husband, for it was Thurlstone himself, cautiously followed them.

A while he stood and watched the 'dark clearly defined outlines of two figures sitting clasped together on the stone seat at the entrance. . . . His wife's arms were entwined round the blind poet's neck, her cheek was pressed fondly to his, and her long dishevelled hair was spread out over his shoulders and round his neck. . . . The great black rock which was suspended over their heads looked as though it were every instant about to fall and crush them for their unconscious sin.

'Helen's husband stood outside in the moonlight, unmindful of the place he was in and the profound obscurity of the abysses under his feet. . . . Everything in outer nature had suddenly lost its existence or reality to him—all his faculties were concentrated on the spectacle before him. . . . The sky was very luminous beyond the dark walls of the cavern: the two heads were as if crowned with a brilliant cluster of stars, some of which appeared to hang like blossoms festooned in Helen's loosened hair as they were seen through its openings. . . . These two lovers, while their minds were involved in the delirious intoxication of reciprocal passion, how little they dreamt what the fulfilment of fate had in store for them! There was no concealment between their hearts; each mingled with free speech in the other's confidence. The man watched them and listened to their enraptured words as though he were paralyzed by his conflicting passions and could only stand there helplessly. At last his constrained inaction became dreadful, contrasted with their freedom. In the darkness and silence of the night it would be impossible to describe how utterly they would be under his power whenever he chose to interrupt them. . . .

'Suddenly, as the man stood there, he heard far off in the distance the measured solemn vibrations of a clock, as it slowly beat out the hour in some remote village belfry . . . what hour it struck was impossible to determine, for the strokes were all mingled together in the one common reverberation which lingered among the rocky hills they passed over. In the disturbed state of his brain it seemed a mysterious indecipherable warning, as from some other long-for-

gotten world which he had once lived in. . . .
One hour nearer the end had sounded. . . .

'This noise, reminding him as it were that other people existed in the world besides the two before him, roused him a little out of his fierce bewilderment. . . . His sun-browned hands were clutched convulsively behind his back, with a kind of nervous twitching in the fingers; one foot was advanced as though he were minded to go to them, did not some irresistible power hold him back. . . .

'He stood full in the light without thought of concealment. If Helen had turned her head she must unfailingly have seen him; if Haenton had listened he might have heard his breathing: but they were too infatuated, too much immersed in themselves for that. . . .

'"Don't you hear the old Countisbury church clock striking? It must be ten. You'll have to lead me home, Arthur, since you know the ground so well, for it's dark all over down below. How secure and happy one feels up here!" said poor Helen, breaking the long and rapturous silence which had lasted between them, with a kind of lingering sigh. There is more meaning in a half-hour's silence between two human beings who love each other than in a whole day's conversation between ordinary men and women. Silence and love are inseparable!'

Then, in the midst of her caresses breaking into song, Helen sang:—

> 'Love is a desultory fire,
>   Blown by a wind made musical with sighs;
>   A void and wonderfully vague desire,
>   Which comes and flies.
>
> 'Of once-sown passion who knows what the crop is?
>   Alas! my love, love's eyes are very blind.
>   What would they have us do?  Sunflowers and poppies
>   Stoop with the wind.'

' "Oh, Haenton," proceeds the heroine, "what a bitter, bitter mockery the unknown love I always bore for you made my marriage seem to me! . . . I half forgot your very existence; but I never forgot for one instant the passion that always slumbered so restlessly in my heart, even if I did not know what I yearned for. It all burst into flame at last, when I saw you. . . I often wondered what I had been made for till then."

'If Helen had looked back through the rocks, she would have seen a man pressing his hands over his face, as though to shut out some sight he dared not look upon.' But Helen did not look, and proceeded with her caresses, all the while recounting the reasons why she had married Thurlstone, for whom, so she averred, she never really cared, and to whom she had engaged herself in a moment of impulse. After these confessions she was proceeding to sing one of her lover's songs, when she suddenly stopped, startled by the deep baying of a dog. With her arm still about Haenton's neck, Helen half rose and turned round. Doing so, and still listening in a startled way, she caught sight of the man's figure; she must have recognised him instantly, for she greeted him with a bewildered scream.

'"Ay, it's my dog, Helen. We've both been half-drowned, but we've come home again: he has been very faithful to me, but then, you see, he's only a dumb animal." He said this with a great effort to articulate calmly, which was very evident. . . . "Who's that man there?" . . .

'There was dignity in Thurlstone's voice and figure as he stood there. Nothing in the world is more ennobling than an unmerited injury. Mrs. Thurlstone had started up suddenly, and with an instinctive effort to conceal her lover behind her dress and hands, and even her hair. It was terrible.

'As her husband spoke, she gave a second shrill cry or scream, like that of a despairing animal, and passed over the fragment of rock they had been sitting on, so as to keep herself in front of the blind man. . . .

'"Spare him, oh spare him! He is not a man like you. I placed myself under your direction, I know, and I am weak as only a woman is; but if you touch one hair of his head, oh God, you shall rue it! . . . How was I to guess you were coming back from the jaws of death to blast the only happiness I care for in life?" . . .

'"And this is all the return you give me for all the years of love I have wasted on you! You tell me to my face that I destroy your happiness," the man interrupted in a wild strident voice that rang sharply among the rocks, while he made a step towards her. She recoiled from him, but it was only to get more in front of Haenton. As her husband stood looking on her, he seemed for an instant about to catch her up in his arms, but the impulse left him.

'"Look you!" said Thurlstone, with a deep and quivering voice. "I love you still, Helen, come what may, so I won't give you any opportunity for inventing lies. . . . Either you come home with me to Waters-meet—follow me now—or by the heaven above us. . . . I'll cast the blind man there off this summit on to the sea-rocks! Will you come quietly, Helen, or not?

Take your choice . . . . no one could blame or punish me, I know very well, and I don't care if they can ! . . ."

' " Oh, I shall go mad ! My heart's bursting !" was all she said: she stood irresolutely for a moment, and then burst into tears. Perhaps the poor girl's imagination pictured a little swirl of blood staining the sea-water below, for, still shuddering, she made a movement as though she would consent to follow her husband. She cast an imploring look behind her to where she had left her lover, and seemed to be about to speak, and then stopped, evidently to avoid calling Thurlstone's attention towards him.

' They both stood facing each other still a little while longer. A pair of evil-looking black-feathered birds, seen dimly in the moonlight, were balancing themselves on the angle of the white rock overhead, and twisting their black beaks on one side to gaze down on them. They seemed to be sleepily taking note of what was passing beneath, and croaking drowsy comments to each other. These birds were a couple of ravens, and had probably been disturbed from the nest they had built in one of the clefts; there was something indescribably sinister in their sudden appearance at such a juncture.

" Remember !" said Thurstone sternly, with a

look towards where Haenton was. Helen started again with a shudder, but this time she suppressed any cry she might have uttered. Then they went down the path together, he in front and she following, for she was in deadly fear lest he should turn back if he got between her and her blind lover. The dog went last of all, still smelling the hem of her garment. The last that was plainly seen of them, just before they plunged into the shadow, was a glimpse of Helen's bloodless face turned upwards to where she had left Haenton.'

Arthur Haenton, after causing the rocks to re-echo vainly with Helen's name, was left to grope his way home alone.

Thus far Oliver carried the story of *The Dwale Bluth* himself, and although he never lived to revise and correct it, a very large portion of his manuscript was, doubtless, as it would have been left by its author even after he had completed the work. The great chasm between books three and four would probably have been more artistically bridged over, and many things altered and improved, at any rate in the final chapters. From what was known of his design, at least at one period of its progress, the editors of his works were enabled to furnish a brief analysis of how it was intended *The Dwale Bluth* should end. Helen, watched and guarded by her husband until the restraint upon her excitable temperament produced brain fever, during a paroxysm of the disease that occurred whilst her nurse slept, strangled herself with her hair.

Not to embitter Helen's condition, Arthur Haenton forbore for some days to make inquiries about her of the neighbours, 'who were glad enough to avoid the task of repeating to him the dark whispers that went around. But he wandered about the well-known, well-loved paths he had so often trodden with his love.' Yet he could not long remain ignorant of her fate. Straying along the narrow zigzag footway which was then the only road connecting Lynmouth with the town of Linton on the heights above, Arthur arrived at a place where there was scarcely room for more than two persons to walk abreast: here he met a funeral procession, 'and in the straitness of the way, the blind man had to *feel* the coffin as it was borne by; asking one of the followers whose funeral it was, he was answered, " Mrs. Thurlstone's of the Waters-meet."'

The unfortunate poet wandered about in the wilderness and gloom for three days, and on the night of the third, with strength almost exhausted, he found his way to Linton churchyard, and there, after hours of weary search, came upon a newly-made grave whereon some hand had placed a large spray of *The Dwale Bluth*, the plant which had been so strangely interwoven with Helen's history. 'Arthur, who was dying of inanition, ravenously ate of the berries. They appeased his craving for food, they appeased his longing for death. It was a sacrifice to *her* shade, and *he* was the victim.'

And thus ends *The Dwale Bluth*, the work which its author never lived to complete, but which, despite its fragmentary unfinished nature, is his *chef d'œuvre*. The latter portion is decidedly inferior to the three first books, so replete as they are with genuine unforced pathos and humour, and presenting as they do such faithful presentations of the mingled mirth and misery of life's complexities. If the last book of this romance, needing though it does the author's finishing touches, is full of the passion and misfortune of love, it lacks sadly those inimitable strokes of humour which place the characters of Oliver Serpleton and old Margery among the immortals created by the genius of man.

*DEATH'S FINAL CONQUEST.*

# In a Graveyard.

## 12th November, 1874.

[*Two intimate friends of Oliver Madox Brown spent the night preceding his funeral in talk upon the sad mystery of his early death. The result was the following sonnet and the one given on page* 2, ante, *composed during the drive from the funeral.*]

Farewell to thee and to our dreams farewell—
   Dreams of high deeds and golden days of thine,
   Where once again should Art's twin powers combine—
The painter's wizard-wand, the poet's spell !—
Though Death strikes free, careless of Heaven and Hell—
   Careless of Man—of Love's most lovely shrine—
   Yet must Man speak—must ask of Heaven a sign
That this wild world is God's and all is well.

Last night we mourned thee, cursing eyeless Death,
   Who, sparing sons of Baal and Ashtoreth,
   Must needs slay thee, with all the world to slay ;—
But round this grave the winds of winter say :
'On earth what hath the poet ? An alien breath ;
   Death holds the keys that ope the doors of Day.'

                                              Theodore Watts.

## CHAPTER VIII.

### DEATH'S FINAL CONQUEST.

'Oh reluctantly lingering breath!
Oh longing with sorrow requited!
Oh blossom the storm-winds have blighted,
Deep down in the shadow of death!'
*Stanzas.* OLIVER MADOX BROWN.

IN our analysis of *The Dwale Bluth*, the fact has already been adverted to that its author had made certain alterations in the earlier portions of his romance, in accordance with the suggestion of the *Cornhill's* editor; that subsequently he was reluctantly induced to allow his revised manuscript to be submitted to that gentleman with a probable view to its use in the magazine under his control, and that after it had been retained for some time, it was returned to Oliver without a word of explanation.

The effects of the disappointment, and apparently the method by which it was brought about, seem to have had a most injurious effect upon the young author's highly susceptible organization. Instead of regarding the return of his manuscript as the result of a want of appreciation by one person only, or as capable of explanation on personal or general grounds, the sensitive youth took the affair seriously to heart, and henceforward would appear to have lost confidence in his own powers. After the prospect of getting his books published through Messrs. Smith, Elder and Co.'s co-operation was thus suddenly, unexpectedly, and curtly closed to him, it was noticed that Oliver became dissatisfied with everything that he wrote. His relatives were unable to overlook the fact, although they paid no particular attention to it at the moment, that henceforth he began to tear up his writings, sometimes whole chapters at a time, and became a constant prey to irritation. He could no longer find satisfaction in anything he wrote, yet steadfastly refused all advice or comfort, and declined to allow anyone to see his work, letting 'concealment, like a worm i' the bud,' canker his boyish hopes.

During 1874, besides his occasional work on *Hebditch's Legacy* and *The Dwale Bluth*, he commenced various other stories; one, a short tale connected with his Devonian studies entitled *The Yeth-Hounds*, is founded on the ancient, widely diffused myth that these

> 'Undefinèd sounds
> That come a-swooning over hollow grounds,
> And wither dreamily on barren moors,'—

are the noises made by a spectral huntsman and his hounds, as they urge on their ghostly course in mad pursuit of a demon lady. Into this short and unfinished legendary story Oliver contrived to instil some charming *vraisemblant* spirit of child-life, made the more realistic by its flavouring of local idiom and folk-lore. The prattle of the little ones who were lost on Dartmoor, and were 'cold to th'' backbone, trembling like wet grass-blades,' supplied a very natural setting for the time-honoured legend.

*Dismal Jemmy*, as well as *The Last Story*, dictated during his fatal illness, were both intended by Oliver to illustrate certain phases which he deemed had hitherto been overlooked in the life and aspect of that London which he was born in, lived in, died in, and loved so well, and which he hoped to treat as Balzac had treated Paris. These tales, the fragment of an Irish story, and some few verses besides those cited in the present volume, form, with those works special mention has already been made of, the literary remains of Oliver Madox Brown.

What will chiefly strike the reader in the perusal of Oliver's work, is the intimate and sympathetic knowledge of the life of children and animals which it so prominently displays. His pets were numerous and unusual, his collection including white rats, green frogs, a large toad—which occasionally swallowed one of the frogs, and also contrived to gulp down its own skin after it had carefully divested itself of the superfluous covering and rolled it into a ball —two chameleons, two Japanese salamanders, striped and patched with flame-colour and black, and flies innumerable, which he hatched, if it may be so termed, from gentles, breeding them to serve as reserve food for the other occupants of his menagerie. The rats, well known to the *habitués* of 37, Fitzroy Square, as 'Nolly's rats,' were kept separate from the rest of the collection; they were white, and quite domesticated, at least so far as concerned their owner, at whose call they would come, and along whose arms and shoulders they would scamper familiarly. His long acquaintanceship with these animals, and his close inspection of their habits, stood him in good stead in his literary labours, wherein, indeed, he seems to have rarely hazarded anything of moment not derived from his own or his friends' observation. In *The Black Swan*, for instance, how natural and telling is the discovery of the ship being on fire foreshadowed to Gabriel Denver by the behaviour of the rats:

'Just at that instant, as he sat trying to collect his thoughts, he felt something scramble over his feet, and looking down and into the circle of light near him, he saw two or three rats, emerging from the shadow, cross through the light and hurry into the opposite obscurity again. One stood up in the manner so characteristic of its kind, no matter what danger they may be flying from, rubbing its neck and whiskers carefully with its wet paws; then it deliberately inspected the end of its tail and disappeared after them, followed by others. He could see their keen teeth and fierce little eyes glistening as they caught the light. These animals, usually so watchful, did not appear at all attracted by his movements, and they were evidently scared already, as if in the presence of some greater and common danger; thus they roused Denver's attention in spite of himself; he could not make out what was the matter with them, and had never before noticed a rat in the ship.'

Oliver was never deterred by the prejudices

of ordinary people: rats are dreaded by those who know nothing about them, so he determined to study the manners and customs of the little furry fellows. Toads, again, are held in general abhorrence, therefore Oliver made them an object of his closest personal observation, with what result readers of *The Dwale Bluth* know. After all, however, it must be acknowledged that it was with cats that his most intimate animal friendships were made. He appeared to exercise a peculiar mesmeric attraction over the feline race, not only with domestic, but even with semi-savage members of the family. It is within the knowledge of many that a number of *wild cats* up till recently infested Fitzroy Square, holding high carnival within the railed enclosure. These unfortunate creatures, living on sparrows, or any garbage they could discover, or often starving, prowled about the neighbourhood in a state of desperate warfare with all other beings; every creature's hands, feet, paws, beaks, and claws against them, and their teeth and claws against everything, even against one another. And yet, marvellous to relate, these all-suspicious animals, though avoiding everyone else, were accustomed to near Oliver, and even gambol round him when he entered the Square. Indeed, it is averred that no feline pariah, however miserable or distraught, but would readily entrust itself to the magnetism of his merciful care. It is also remembered that when he was detained one night at a friend's house, the cat at home, which was very fond of him, sat by the street-door, watching for him the whole night through.

Oliver's fondness for children and their ways was doubtless closely connected with his love of animals: the helplessness and dependence of infancy apparently aroused his tenderest interest, and invoked that intense sympathy he reserved chiefly for the unfortunate or powerless. *The Dwale Bluth* is replete with instances of his intimacy with childhood, and evinces a knowledge of child-life rarely paralleled outside the sacred sisterhood of matrons, whilst anecdotes are related by his friends corroborative of the belief that he evinced in actual life that love for infancy, and that susceptibility to its feelings, which his works give evidence of.

His constitutional carelessness about worldly matters has already been adverted to, and it is by no means improbable that a knowledge of his own infirmity was partly accountable for his portraiture of the Rev. Oliver Serpleton's eccentricities, although a living model has been found for that personage. Whether a longer life would have developed this idiosyncrasy into such extremes with our Oliver as with his namesake, it is idle to speculate. In some cases it is possible that he had reasons for his apparently unreasonable habits, as, for instance, when his sister sent him from abroad a spray of the real deadly *Belladonna*, he omitted—perhaps purposely—to avail himself of the opportunity, retaining his own already written less correct, albeit more picturesque, description of the plant. Again, in *Hebditch's Legacy*, having once drawn from his own vivid imagination a description of the banks of the Medway, he positively refused to alter it to one more correct. 'Truth,' we have been informed, 'either from a psychological or pictorial point of view, he revered, but seems to have despised small details of facts.' Certainly he never despised artistic nor picturesque elements, and in *his* mania there was always method. In his personal habits and attire he avoided both foppishness and negligence, and although he detested conventionality, was careful not to develop eccentricities; the only partiality for any particular article he was known to show having been for a large ebony Indian walking-stick, inlaid with ivory, and having a handle shaped somewhat like a bishop's crosier. This stick was the constant and favourite companion of his rambles; it had been given to him by his brother-in-law, Mr. William M. Rossetti, and was doubtless much prized on that account; but it also possessed an artistic, not to say historic, interest that must have enhanced its value in his eyes: previous to the stick having been presented to Oliver, it had been lent to Dante Rossetti, and by him was introduced in the picture of *Marianne*, and then to Ford Madox Brown, who depicted it in his painting of *Joseph's Coat*. Truly a relic to be prized and guarded!

When he was about fourteen or fifteen he commenced wearing glasses, and used them to the end of his life. Somewhere about sixteen he took to smoking, and, at one time, would appear to have indulged somewhat extensively in the habit. His hair was brown, streaked with gold, and was worn parted down the centre. His eyes were grey. When animated, his features assumed a sort of intensified keenness, mingled at times with a sweet playfulness of expression. His habitual uninspired expression was somewhat *blasé*, whilst his customary mode of talk— used as a shield against the commonplace chatter of others—was a mingling of common-sense with contempt for weak enthusiasm.

Oliver was a remarkably fine reader, especially of anything humorous, and Philip Bourke Marston says, 'I shall always remember one night, when I was feeling particularly out of sorts, his coming in and reading the great trial scene out of *Pickwick*. There is no doubt that he had in this line great dramatic capabilities.' He was an ardent admirer of *The City of Dreadful Night*, and read it through one night at Fitzroy Square in company with Mr. Marston, the two sitting up very late in order to accomplish the perusal.

'He gave to his work,' says Mr. Marston, 'all that love and devotion that a great artist gives to a great art; he probably possessed more than any writer of the present time that complete objectivity, not requisite to the poet, but indispensable to the dramatist and novelist. It was difficult to satisfy him with his own work; he would frequently, when half-way through a story, without a regret cast aside all he had done, and write it afresh.

'Of his conscientious method of working you may form some idea when I tell you that the walls of his room, in which he habitually wrote, were covered with sheets of paper containing some hundreds of names collected from different sources, which were to pass before him in review, till he lighted on such names as he deemed suitable to his character.'

Oliver possessed a fairly large collection of

books, with the contents of which he seems to have been thoroughly acquainted. The poets were his favourite authors, but at first hand, or through the medium of translation, he managed not only to peruse the chief masterpieces of English and foreign *Belles Lettres*, but, also, much that was curious and *outré*: indeed, his library was a medley of all sorts of 'odds and ends,' gathered together with a view to becoming, one day or another, useful aids to the working out of his imagination. It was his custom to read a book directly after he had purchased it.

'I may say,' writes Mr. Marston, 'that all who knew him loved him. He was the best and truest of friends, possessing a nature warm and sympathetic; yet I never knew any occasion on which his friendship dimmed his sense of justice. More than once I have benefited by his keen intellect, which often detected my wrong from right, as I afterwards came to see. Had he lived, he would have developed into one of those men to whom other men in their sore need look for strength and counsel. His standard of life was a high one. I remember how once, for nearly an hour, he talked almost uninterruptedly, to show me how large an influence man has on the world, by simply living out his life to its highest possibilities. That night he was in one of his gravest and most thoughtful moods. His conversation generally was quick with *repartée*, which sometimes hurt just a little; but his bright smile and cordial shake of the hand always healed instantly the slight wound which his tongue might have unwittingly caused.

'He was free from the slightest trace of sentimentality; his nature was essentially masculine and robust, having that almost maternal tenderness which in noble natures is generally coupled with strength. His friendship evinced itself in those little acts of consideration and tact which help so materially to sweeten life. It was, moreover, equal to the highest test, as I have personal reasons for knowing.'

Notwithstanding the fact that during the last few months Oliver must have frequently endured severe bodily suffering, and that his imaginative susceptibility caused him to feel deeply the editorial rejection of his last romance, his life on the whole was one of much happiness. As Mr. Marston has said: 'During his brief and remarkable life he enjoyed the friendship of some of the most distinguished men of his time, who yielded him their admiration with no stint.' The idol of his relatives and many friends; the author, whilst still in his teens, of a popular and much applauded romance; known as a clever artist and a true poet, and with no real worldly cares to cumber his mind, he must have enjoyed no small share of earthly happiness. He was spared the misery of manhood and the apathetic despair of old age, living only long enough to taste the unsatiating pleasure of youth.

His various attacks of ill-health had not created any particular anxiety among his relatives. In September, 1874, however, he was too unwell, suffering from gout in the foot, to accompany the various members of his family to Margate. An extra bedroom, nevertheless, was taken for him, and he was shortly expected to rejoin the party at the sea-side, little or no danger being apprehended. On the 15th of the month he wrote to his friend Marston:

'37, Fitzroy Square.
DEAR PHILIP,
You asked me to write and tell you how I felt when I should reach home. I have been very bad, and can hardly hold my pen even now. I luckily found a cab at the corner in the Hampstead Road, or I don't know how I should have got home at all—and I have had a violent pain in my side ever since, which has something to do with enlargement of the liver, I am told, by way of encouragement. Cheerful this! I am going

down to Margate to-morrow, if well enough, which I have my doubts of, and so expect I shall not see you for some time to come. So you see I was really ill for once in a way, maugre your scepticism—which is some faint consolation after all, I take it. Believe me, till we meet again,

Affectionately yours,

O. Madox Brown.'

On the morrow, however, Oliver was still too unwell to leave home, and on the 19th, being yet detained by his failing health, he wrote the following (his last) letter to his dear friend:—

'37, Fitzroy Square.

Dear P. B. M.,

I am still laid up and grievously afflicted by the Lord—to whom, etc., etc., etc. The family are all departed, however, as it was necessary for my sister that they should wait no longer. I hope to be able to rejoin them in a few days. But for the present I have to content myself with a minute survey of a newly white-washed ceiling I have the honour of sleeping under of nights, and with saying my prayers, as I am quite alone. I am not blasphemous at heart—contrarywise, I am truly reverential; but I wish I could control creation for a little while.

. . . . What I want to ask is whether you could by any possibility call and spend a few hours here to-morrow—Saturday. I should be only too glad to see you, if you will send a line to say you can beforehand. Only be sure not to come unless I send you a telegram in the course of the day saying I am really ready to see you. I am writing in bed, so please excuse spelling and handwriting, and believe me,

    Always yours,
      OLIVER MADOX BROWN.'

His health appeared to improve, and he rejoined his relatives at the sea-side, but was never really enabled to throw off the hectic fever which had followed the attack of rheumatic gout. Within a week he returned to London without having derived any benefit from his journey, and again took to his bed. The fatal malady from which he was suffering ultimately developed into pyæmia, or blood-poisoning. 'Full of energy, of hope, of noble aspirations, with "mountains of work" before him,' says the critic in the article already cited from, 'the most promising young man perhaps of our time—the most variously endowed, surely—was one day crossed in his path by an enemy unseen and little recked —a poison gemmule floating in the air, and merely seeking a nidus, just as the young poet himself was seeking his goal—the goal to which he was to devote his life; and in a week or two Oliver Madox Brown is but a memory!'

During the progress of his final illness Oliver either read or dictated. The *Last Story*, the fragment of a tale of London life already alluded to, was taken down from the dying lad's lips, partly by his mother and partly by his brother-in-law, Mr. William M. Rossetti. 'Wasted and exhausted as he was with fever,' writes Mr. Rossetti, 'the brain still worked, though the hand was incapable of holding the pen.' And it was his long cherished thought of popularizing and making better known the hidden secrets of the mighty metropolis that still swayed the last scintillations of the lad's powerful mind. With what fidelity to fact and with what vigour did the dying youth portray the misery of young children of the lowest classes of the earth's wealthiest city. 'How we children managed to live up our ally,' is the supposed autobiographical record of the hero of the *Last Story*, 'swarming as we were, God alone knows! It is not often that one of us survives to attain any other position save that of a dwarfed and beery imbecility. But the faculties are sharpened like those of rats: not the slightest thing eatable wedged into the crannies of the pavement or splashed upon the wall; no piece of carrot or end of cabbage-leaf, can possibly elude our attention. We swarm and live like animals —it almost seems as though on one another. I remember I often used to sit watching the sparrows on the parapets, wondering whether they were as hungry as I, convincing myself that they were not, and even feeling jealous of them. .... The children I lived amongst were simply like rats. We neither bit nor choked each other ; but if any piece of garbage had been flung suddenly up the alley, we should have fought each other wildly for it with our teeth and nails.'

Even this slight fragment of a fragment, divested, too, of all its interest and *vraisemblance*, as it necessarily is, when standing by itself, proves the vitality of the author's intellect up to within a few days of his death, and that had he been spared to fulfil his purpose of writing a tale of London life of the very lowest class— with the intention of its being serious and pathetic, in contradistinction to the habit of representing these classes from the ridiculous point of view, something new but true, and worthy of the highest aims of Fiction, might have been given to the world. But it was not to be, for, as his friend Marston wrote, 'A wonderful future lay in front; but before the strong heart and brain could weary on the way, Death withdrew him.' The sad, strange, but too truthful tableaux of children in police-courts, gin-sodden females fighting in barely habitable dens, and infants kicked, spurned, and starved by the authors of their existence, which the dying youth described, are only faint sketches of what, had fate been more propitious, would have proved imperishable masterpieces of our literature.

Whilst on his death-bed Oliver became acquainted with Mr. Blackmore's *Lorna Doone*, a novel dealing with that same Devonshire scenery he had described in his own romance of *The Dwale Bluth*. Over and over again the poor youth read the book, thinking, doubtless, of his own unfinished and unpublished work. And during this last wasting illness he read or had read to him the first chapters of *Far from the Madding Crowd*, as they appeared in the *Cornhill Magazine*, and after coming to that where Gabriel Oak cares for the young lambs through the winter night, he generously exclaimed, 'No wonder they did not want *my* writing!' alluding to the non-acceptance of *The Dwale Bluth* by the editor of the periodical in which Mr. Hardy's tale was publishing.

For five weeks Oliver lay wasting away from the fatal blood-poisoning, the cause of which has never been discovered, until, as his brother-in-law says, 'the once healthy and active youth had become but a trembling hectic incurable, bereft of hearing, and without hope from medical aid. Acute pain had, after a while, given way to feverous restlessness, as this in turn was to be succeeded by delirium.' And so the end came, and the young life, the flush of hope and youth still full upon it, faded away. It was on the 5th of November, the anniversary of the publication of *Gabriel Denver*—that 'night of all nights in the year'—the spirit of its youthful author passed away. Well might Dante Rossetti write to the father *then*, 'Alas, alas! what can one say? Is it lost everywhere as here? If so, there is neither gain nor loss in anything, for all is dross.'

But with the forethought of one acquainted with grief—when on the twelfth of the weary month the earthly remains of their beloved one were consigned to the bosom of the universal mother—Mr. Moncure D. Conway said to the parents and sisters: 'At length, wintry as this grave now seems, grass will cover it and flowers bloom over it; and over the deeper wounds in hearts the healing hand of Time will bring the softening growths: it may be even flowers in the end.'

And now it is even so: the grass has grown and the flowers have blossomed, and the prophetic words of Oliver's friend Philip are fulfilling:—

> 'But though he has gone out from us, his name
> Shall lessen not with time, and his young fame
> Shall burn for ever, an enduring flame,
> A steadfast light that may not wax or wane.'

THE END.

ELLIOT STOCK, LONDON.

# ELLIOT STOCK'S PUBLICATIONS.

In small 4to, on antique paper, price 15s., post free.

## *Sonnets of Three Centuries:*

*A Representative Collection of the Best English Sonnets from Spenser to the present day.*

Embodying many Inedited and hitherto Unpublished Examples. The whole Arranged Chronologically, and accompanied by Illustrative Notes and a Copious Historical and Bibliographical Introduction, by T. HALL CAINE.

'The beautiful volume before us is, beyond all doubt, the most satisfactory collection of sonnets that has yet appeared.'—*Athenæum.*

'The get-up of this book, as to paper, type, and size, is almost ideal.'—*Notes and Queries.*

---

Now ready, in post 8vo, with a Portrait, price 7s. 6d., post free.

## *Recollections of Dante Gabriel Rossetti.*

### By T. HALL CAINE.

'The book is one which no one who has English literature at heart should fail to study.'—*Academy.*
'The work is likely to be much read.'—*Daily News.*
'Mr. Caine has furnished a pleasant book.'—*Athenæum.*

---

In crown 8vo, cloth elegant, price 2s. 6d.

## *Dante Gabriel Rossetti,*

*His Work and Influence, including a Brief Survey of Recent Art Tendencies.*

### By WILLIAM TIREBUCK.

'Mr. Tirebuck's essay must be read as an appreciative monograph, written wholly from an independent standpoint; and as such it will doubtless find many readers among those who are anxious to acquire information, however indirect, touching the most fascinating personality of the age.'—*Academy.*

ELLIOT STOCK'S PUBLICATIONS.

In crown 8vo, cloth extra, price 5s., post free.

## *The Human Inheritance; The New Hope; Motherhood.*

By WILLIAM SHARP.

'The reader will be arrested and refreshed by their noticeable originality and by a spirit of pure virile strength which characterizes every poem in the collection. We shall look forward with great interest to another volume from the pen of Mr. Sharp. In the meanwhile we feel assured that a new name, destined to become conspicuous, has been added to the ranks of our nineteenth century poets.'—*Morning Post.*

---

In crown 8vo, cloth elegant, price 4s. 6d., post free.

## *The New Medusa, and other Poems.*

By EUGENE LEE-HAMILTON, Author of 'Gods, Saints, and Men,' etc.

'There can be no doubt that the author is a true poet.'—*Graphic.*

'We should have to go to great names among contemporary poets before we found a volume of verse with a message so clear and so touching.'—*Athenæum.*

---

Now ready, crown 8vo, price 4s. 6d.

## *Poems and Lyrics.*

By LOUISA S. BEVINGTON, Author of 'Key Notes.'

'There is a certain force in it that makes us all desire to read more. . . . . Miss Bevington has on the whole produced a volume of promising verse.'—*Public Opinion.*

---

In crown 8vo, cloth elegant, price 4s. 6d., post free.

## *Verses of Varied Life.*

By H. T. MACKENZIE BELL, Author of 'The Keeping of the Vow,' etc.

'His verses bear witness to considerable powers of observation, a liberal education, and some capacity for original thought.'—*Academy.*

---

LONDON: ELLIOT STOCK, 62, PATERNOSTER ROW, E.C.

www.ingramcontent.com/pod-product-compliance
Lightning Source LLC
Chambersburg PA
CBHW032223230426
43666CB00033B/749